ST. THERESE LENDING LIBRARY

FBI

ST. THERESE LENDING LIBRARY

FBI

BY MELVIN BERGER

◄— A FIRST BOOK —►
FRANKLIN WATTS | NEW YORK | LONDON | 1977

Cover design by Al Cetta

Photographs courtesy of
the Federal Bureau of Investigation

Library of Congress Cataloging in Publication Data

Berger, Melvin.
    FBI.

    (A First book)
    Bibliography: p.
    Includes index.
    SUMMARY: Discusses the history of the FBI, training and work of Special Agents, and the operation of the FBI Laboratory and Identification Division.
    1. United States. Federal Bureau of Investigation — Juvenile literature. 2. Criminal investigation — United States — Juvenile literature. [1. United States. Federal Bureau of investigation. 2. Criminal investigation] I. Title.
HV8141.B4   364.12′06′173   77-1395
ISBN 0-531-01285-9

Copyright © 1977 by Melvin Berger
All rights reserved
Printed in the United States of America
5 4 3 2

CONTENTS

THE CASE OF THE
NEW JERSEY MAYOR
1

HISTORY OF THE FBI
6

THE MEN AND WOMEN
OF THE FBI
15

SPECIAL AGENTS AT WORK
25

THE FBI LAB
34

IDENTIFICATION DIVISION
49

FURTHER READING
62

INDEX
64

ACKNOWLEDGMENTS

Many men and women of the FBI helped me in the writing of this book. I am grateful to them all. I would like, however, to express my particular gratitude to: Clarence M. Kelley, Director; Donald W. Moore, Jr., Assistant Director; and Buz Howell, Special Agent of the Washington, D.C., Headquarters of the FBI; Ronald E. Young, Press Officer, New York City Field Office; and to Richard D. Rogge, Special Agent in Charge; Joseph J. Ross, Jr., Assistant Special Agent in Charge; and Garry G. Lash, Special Agent of the Buffalo, New York, Field Office.

THE CASE OF THE NEW JERSEY MAYOR

The mayor of a large New Jersey city walked into the FBI office. He glanced around the nearly empty room. There were several desks, with clear tops, neatly lined up in a row. Most of the FBI Special Agents, though, were absent. They were out on their cases. Only two Special Agents were at their desks. One of them put down the papers he was reading to greet the visitor.

The Special Agent was dressed in a business suit and tie. There was no sign of a uniform or of a gun; no special hat or badge. In fact, he looked more like a middle-aged lawyer or a stockbroker than a crime fighter.

The mayor and the Special Agent sat down at the Agent's desk. The mayor began his story:

Joey D., the head of a large electrical supply house, had offered him a bribe of $400,000 to approve a new shopping center in the city. Many people, including the mayor, were opposed to the shopping center. They believed that the new center would force small stores in the neighborhood out of business. It would ruin the character of the area. However, the mayor had told Joey D. that he would think it over. Now he wanted the Special Agent to advise him what to do.

The Agent questioned the mayor closely. He tried to learn as much as he could about what had been said. He made careful notes on the mayor's account of the attempted bribe.

Then he outlined his plan to obtain proof of the bribe. "We need your permission to record conversations on your telephone," the Agent said to the mayor. "We would like a record of Joey's phone calls to you. If you approve, I'll send someone up to your office right away with a tape recorder. Make sure no one sees him. If Joey calls, make an appointment to meet him in a public place."

The mayor signed the necessary papers and went back to his office. In a few hours, an FBI communications expert arrived. He attached a recorder to the mayor's City Hall telephone. A wire led from the recorder to an automatic tape recorder hidden in a desk drawer.

Joey called the next day. The conversation was recorded on tape. According to instructions from the FBI, the mayor arranged to meet Joey at a large, busy restaurant the following evening.

Before the meeting, the FBI communications expert came to see the mayor again. This time, he taped a tiny flat microphone to the mayor's chest. The wires were hidden under the mayor's jacket. They ran from the microphone to a miniature tape recorder. The recorder was in the mayor's trouser pocket.

"Get all the information you can," the FBI Agent told the mayor. "Find out if Joey is acting alone or with others. Try to make an appointment with the top man, if there is one. We'll be watching from another table in the restaurant."

The mayor played his part well. He got more details on the deal. He learned that Arthur S., a businessman with connections in organized crime, was the man behind the bribe. He asked Joey to introduce him to Arthur. The mayor and Joey decided to meet with Arthur for a Sunday morning breakfast, the following week.

Early that Sunday morning, the office of the FBI was busy and noisy. About twenty Agents were in the room. Presently the Agent in Charge of the case called everyone together. They seated themselves around him in the center of the room.

Two of the Agents looked like well-dressed older women on their way to church. One couple was dressed for tennis. Several bearded younger men wore jeans and work shirts. Three men were in fishing garb. The rest wore ordinary street clothes.

While the Agent in Charge gave instructions for covering the meeting in the diner, the communications expert was getting the mayor ready. He fitted him with a microphone and a radio transmitter. This device would allow FBI Agents, some distance away, to hear the conversation as it took place. He taped the radio transmitter, the size of a pack of cigarettes, inside the mayor's trousers; the sensitive microphone, he placed in His Honor's belt buckle.

The mayor, Joey, and Arthur sat around a table in the diner. Glancing around the room, the mayor saw the disguised FBI Agents seated at various other places. The Agents gave no sign that they knew him.

As Arthur raised his bribe offer to $500,000 and pressed the mayor to agree to the terms, the FBI Agents inside the diner filmed the scene with tiny hidden cameras. Other Agents, seated in a van parked outside the diner, recorded the entire conversation on tape. When the mayor finally agreed, they went out to the parking lot, where Joey handed him a large folder containing a first payment of $100,000.

Later, the mayor turned the money over to the Agents. Together with the photographs, the recordings, and their reports, it made up the evidence that they gave the United States Attorney.

The new FBI building located in Washington, D.C.

It was enough evidence to obtain warrants for the arrests of Joey and Arthur.

FBI Agents arrested both men at their homes. They both surrendered peacefully.

Joey and Arthur pleaded guilty to the charge of bribery. They gave the names of others involved in the scheme. A total of seven defendants were brought to trial. All were found guilty, and all were sentenced to terms in prison.

This is just one of the thousands of cases that are solved every year by the FBI.

The FBI, or Federal Bureau of Investigation, is a part of the Department of Justice of the United States government. Orders from the president or the attorney general and laws from Congress direct the FBI to investigate, or find the facts, in many different kinds of crimes. They range from offering a bribe to a government official, to bank robbery, kidnaping, bombing, spying, and hijacking. Also included are crimes in which a criminal or stolen goods cross a state line, and serious crimes on government land or against government property.

Investigations of these crimes lead the FBI to some of the most violent and dangerous criminals in the United States. Yet the FBI is not a cops-and-robbers organization. FBI Agents solve most of their cases without ever firing a shot, or even taking their guns from their holsters. Heavily armed criminals, facing long prison terms, will usually surrender without a fight when captured by FBI Agents.

Today's crimes are different from those being committed even a few years ago. Today's FBI is finding new and different ways to solve these crimes. In FBI offices all over the country, a wonderful new chapter in the history of this world-famous crime-fighting force is being written.

HISTORY OF THE FBI

The FBI started in 1908 as a tiny division within the Justice Department of the United States government. The men in the division investigated various cases for the Justice Department. They searched for evidence, they collected facts and figures, and they questioned suspects and witnesses. They wrote reports to help Justice Department lawyers bring the cases to court.

During World War I, the bureau was given the job of protecting the country from foreign spies. At the war's end, they were also asked to investigate crimes involving stolen cars that had been driven across state lines.

In 1924, J. Edgar Hoover was named Director of the bureau. He held this post for nearly forty-eight years, until his death in 1972. Under Hoover, the bureau grew vastly in size and power, as the number of federal crimes it investigated began to expand.

When Hoover took control of the bureau, there was growing lawlessness throughout the land. Crime was widespread. Gangs of hoodlums were involved in gambling and illegal liquor operations. Professional killers could be hired to commit murder for

J. Edgar Hoover, first director of the FBI (1924-1972)

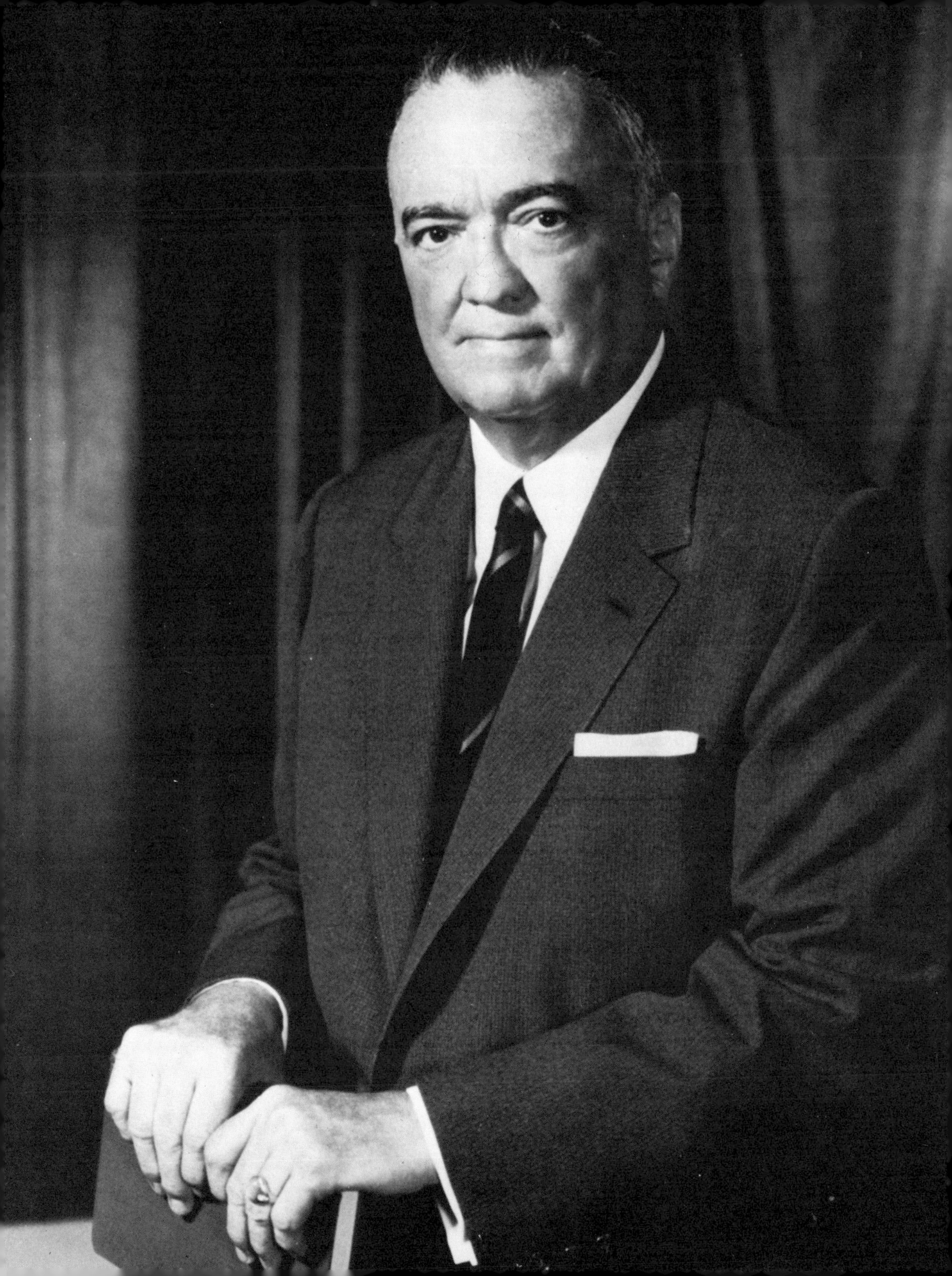

money. There were waves of murders, robberies, kidnapings, and other violent crimes.

Hoover and the Agents of the FBI worked to control this outbreak of crime. While joining with police officers in the capture of Machine Gun Kelly in Memphis, Tennessee, in September 1933, the FBI Agents acquired their nickname. As Kelly came out of his hiding place with his hands above his head he cried out, "Don't shoot, G-men!" The word *G-men* (for government men) caught on, and has been attached to FBI Agents from then on.

The following year, 1934, FBI agents captured or killed several dangerous gang leaders, the so-called public enemies. Among them were John Dillinger, Pretty Boy Floyd, and Baby Face Nelson. In 1935, Ma and Fred Barker were killed in a gun battle that lasted 4½ hours. With these public enemies either dead or behind bars, the gangster era came to an end.

The start of World War II in 1941 changed the work of the FBI. Its most important job, now, was to protect the country from spies and saboteurs who were trying to steal military secrets and to interfere with the war effort.

The most spectacular case came in 1942, when a German submarine landed two groups of saboteurs on America's eastern coast. One group of four came ashore on Long Island; the other group near Jacksonville, Florida. All of them were highly trained. They came to blow up factories that were manufacturing war materials. They also planned to bomb railroad stations through which troop trains were passing. If not checked, these German saboteurs would have spread terror in many big cities of the United States. But, within two weeks, before any damage had been done, the FBI was able to capture all eight saboteurs.

GEORGE R. KELLY
ALIAS "MACHINE GUN KELLY"

- KIDNAPER.
- PARTICIPATED IN URSCHEL KIDNAPING ON JULY 22, 1933.
- APPREHENDED ON SEPTEMBER 26, 1933, IN MEMPHIS, TENNESSEE, BY FBI AGENTS.
- FIRST CRIMINAL TO CALL FBI AGENTS "G-MEN"
- CONVICTED AND SENTENCED TO LIFE IMPRISONMENT.
- DIED IN PENITENTIARY IN 1954.

JOHN DILLINGER

- LEADER OF DILLINGER GANG.
- NOTORIOUS OUTLAW, BANK ROBBER AND GANGSTER.
- LED A REIGN OF TERROR THROUGHOUT THE MIDWEST, ROBBING BANKS IN HALF A DOZEN STATES.
- KILLED IN CHICAGO, ILLINOIS, ON JULY 22, 1934, BY FBI AGENTS WHEN HE RESISTED ARREST.

CHARLES ARTHUR FLOYD
ALIAS "PRETTY BOY FLOYD"

- HIGHWAY ROBBER, BANK ROBBER AND KILLER.
- PARTICIPATED IN KANSAS CITY MASSACRE, JUNE 17, 1933.
- HE WAS KILLED ON OCTOBER 22, 1934, BY FBI AGENTS AND LOCAL POLICE OFFICERS NEAR EAST LIVERPOOL, OHIO, WHILE RESISTING ARREST.

"BABY FACE NELSON"
ALIAS OF LESTER J. GILLIS

- MEMBER OF DILLINGER GANG.
- KILLER AND BANK ROBBER IN MIDWEST.
- DURING HIS CRIMINAL CAREER NELSON KILLED 3 FBI AGENTS.
- NELSON WAS KILLED IN A GUN BATTLE WITH FBI AGENTS ON NOVEMBER 27, 1934, AT BARRINGTON, ILLINOIS.

KATE BARKER
ALIAS "MA" BARKER

- LEADER OF BARKER-KARPIS GANG.
- SHE GUIDED HER 4 SONS, FRED, HERMAN, LLOYD AND "DOC" BARKER INTO CAREERS OF CRIME.
- "MA" BARKER AND SON, FRED, WERE KILLED IN GUN BATTLE WITH FBI AGENTS ON JANUARY 16, 1935, AT OKLAWAHA, FLORIDA.

Hardly had the shooting of World War II ended, when the Cold War began. The late 1940s and 1950s were a time of very poor relations between the Soviet Union and the United States. The Soviet system of communism clashed with the American capitalist system. With great zeal, the FBI undertook to fight the so-called communist menace. They attempted to find communist spies from abroad, as well as identify members and supporters of the Communist party at home.

The 1960s ushered in a period of friendship between the Soviet Union and the United States. But there was a great deal of unrest at home. There were civil rights demonstrations, rallies against the war in Vietnam, and student protests on high school and college campuses. Some extremists set off bombs and used other terrorist methods to call attention to their demands. The FBI set out to prevent these outbursts of violence.

During the 1960s and early 1970s, the FBI went all out to capture those who committed acts of violence, and to learn of future activities. In 1976, there were reports that some FBI Agents had been allowed to use illegal methods in those investigations. It was said that records of radical organizations had been obtained illegally, rather than with proper search warrants. There were also charges of spying on people, of taps on their telephones, even of Agents physically attacking and kidnaping some of the leaders of radical groups. Also, several officials of the FBI were accused of misusing bureau property and the services of bureau employees.

Clarence M. Kelley, Director of the bureau since his appointment by President Nixon in 1973, took on the job of investigating these charges. He set out to correct the abuses in the bureau. Mr. Kelley had been a Special Agent of the FBI for twenty years.

William Webster, Director of the FBI since early 1978, in his official portrait.

After his retirement, he became chief of police in Kansas City, Missouri, for twelve years. He left that position when he was named Director of the FBI.

Director Kelley collected information on past illegal activities in the bureau. He took measures to make sure that FBI Agents, now and in the future, would not commit crimes as they tried to control crime.

In a speech that he delivered in May, 1976, Director Kelley spoke about the suspected illegal FBI activities of the '60s and '70s. He said: "Some of these activities were clearly wrong and quite indefensible. We most certainly must never allow them to be repeated.... We are truly sorry we were responsible for instances which now are subject to such criticism."

The final point Director Kelley made in his speech was: "It is time for the FBI's critics to concentrate on the FBI present and the FBI future. Yes, there have been errors, but I say it is time to permit the FBI and all peace-keeping agencies to get on with their mission."

The present and future mission of the FBI is to investigate and solve crimes — as it has always been. But now FBI Agents must follow new rules and guidelines that are being set up. These new provisions assure more protection of the rights of all people, crime suspects and others, who are under investigation by the FBI.

As the questions and doubts that surround the FBI are cleared up, the bureau is turning more of its attention to the changing pattern of crime in America. The gangsters of the 1930s, the spies of the 1940s, the communists of the 1950s, and the often unlawful mobs of demonstrators of the 1960s are no longer big threats. White-collar crime, like forgery, and organized crime, like illegal gambling, are the fastest-growing types of criminal activity.

The FBI has already changed its crime-fighting methods to meet this new challenge. They are succeeding in the struggle against these new kinds of crimes. From the upset and change of the mid-1970s, a new and better FBI is emerging.

THE MEN AND WOMEN OF THE FBI

The FBI is a nationwide organization of about twenty thousand men and women. The center of this vast network is the FBI Headquarters, a large, new building in Washington, D.C. Here are the offices of the Director and other top officials. Here, too, are the scientific laboratory, the computers, and the fingerprint identification files where many of the technical experts of the FBI work. Helping them are the clerical workers who do the many jobs that are necessary for the smooth running of the FBI.

The investigations which are the main responsibility of the FBI are done by the Special Agents. (Often they are just called Agents.) There are about eighty-five hundred Special Agents in the bureau. Most of them are found in the fifty-nine large Field Offices of the bureau. These offices are located only in the biggest cities. A large city may have hundreds of Agents; a smaller city, a few dozen Agents. An average Field Office has about one hundred Special Agents.

The Special Agents who do not work in Field Offices work out of the Resident Agencies. There are about five hundred Resident Agencies throughout the country. They are located in small cities and towns from coast to coast. Each one is staffed with only a few Special Agents.

Most of the Special Agents are men. Only sixty or so are women; but their numbers are growing. Women Agents are given the same training as men. They perform the same duties and have the same responsibilities as the male Agents.

Each year the bureau accepts several hundred applications from men and women who wish to become Special Agents. Applicants must be citizens of the United States and between the ages of twenty-three and thirty-five. They must have good vision and hearing, and be in excellent physical condition. They must also hold college degrees in either law or accounting. Some applicants are accepted with other degrees if they have experience in fields that will help them become good Agents. Still others are accepted with a degree in science or foreign languages for certain positions.

Every applicant must pass a written test and an oral interview. Also, the applicant must receive the highest personal character recommendations from teachers, ministers, friends, neighbors, and others.

A man or woman who meets the requirements, passes the tests, and gets the needed references is invited to become a recruit at the FBI Academy, located on the grounds of the Marine Corps base in Quantico, Virginia. The Academy, which is about one hour's drive from Washington, D.C., has eleven modern, collegelike buildings. They include classrooms, a library, gymnasium, dining room, and dormitories. The recruits sleep on narrow cots, two to a room.

The recruits are divided into classes of about thirty each for the fifteen-week course of study. Each class has a counselor from the Academy to advise and help the recruits.

Studies at the FBI Academy are more difficult than studies at

The FBI Academy in Quantico, Virginia, where Agents receive their initial training.

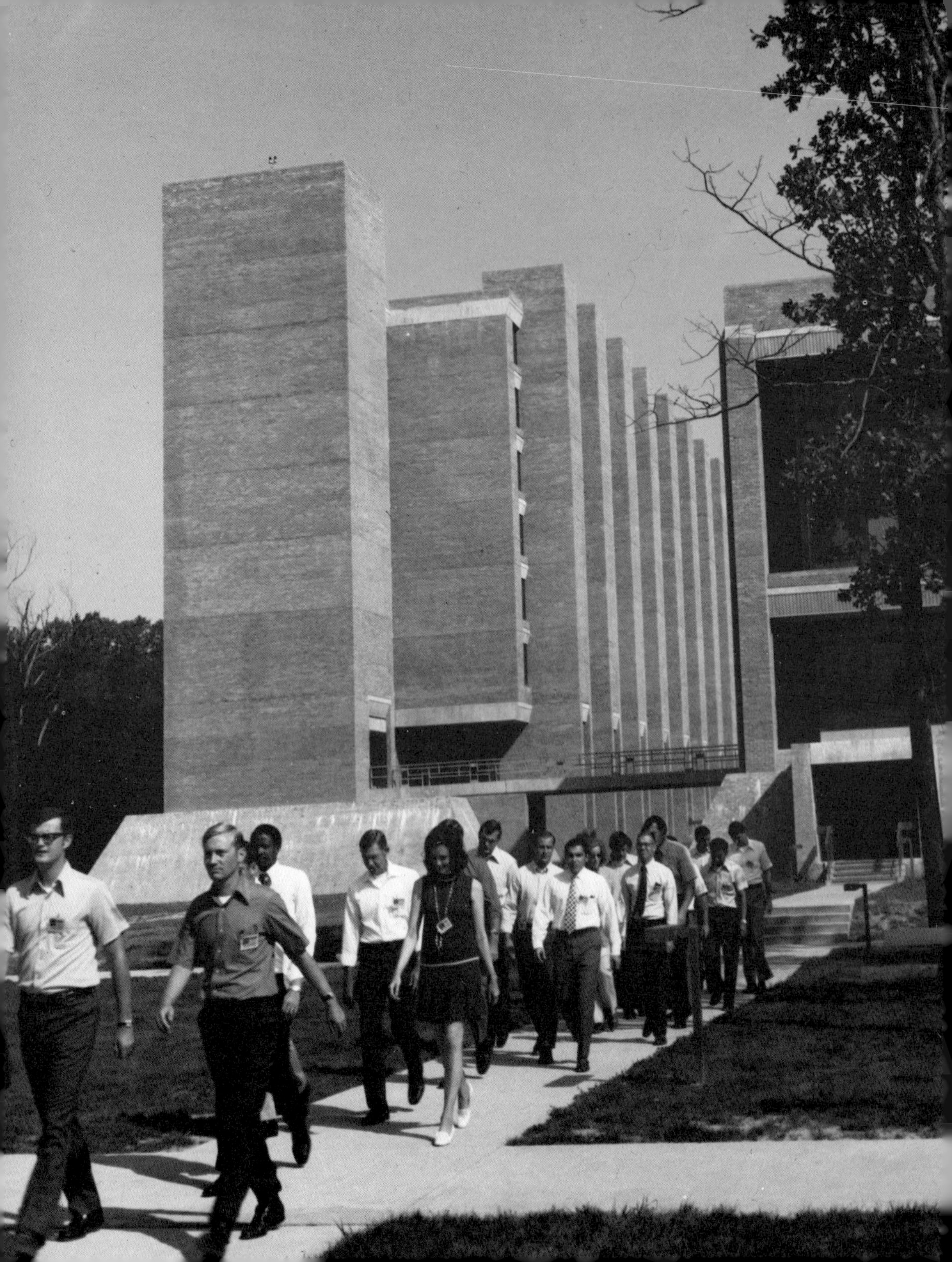

most colleges. The recruits attend classes Monday through Friday, from eight in the morning until five in the afternoon. Then they do their homework until late at night and on weekends.

Recruits study law. They get to know the federal laws that they will enforce, laws concerning the power to search and arrest, recent Supreme Court decisions, and so on. They study psychology. They need to learn how to deal with suspects, victims, and witnesses; and how to handle difficult situations. They find out how the bureau operates. They learn how to fill out the many reports and forms that are part of all investigations.

The students attend lectures given by experts in the field of criminal investigation: How to Rescue a Hostage; Ways to Investigate a Bank Robbery; Collecting and Identifying Fingerprints; White-Collar Crimes That Use Computers; Working With the Local Police. These are some of the sample topics.

Physical training is an important part of the life of a recruit. Everyone works to build up his or her physical condition. Every few weeks the recruit is tested. Push-ups, pull-ups, swimming, two-mile run, and rope climbing are some of the skills that are practiced. There is also instruction and practice in hand-to-hand combat, and searching, disarming, and handcuffing a suspect.

After four weeks or so, the recruit begins to spend considerable time on the firing range. Many of the recruits have never fired a gun. They learn how to handle revolvers, rifles, and shotguns. They practice firing at varying distances from the target, and in different positions. They become expert in drawing and firing quickly, and aiming accurately. FBI Special Agents are

A class of Special Agents in training.

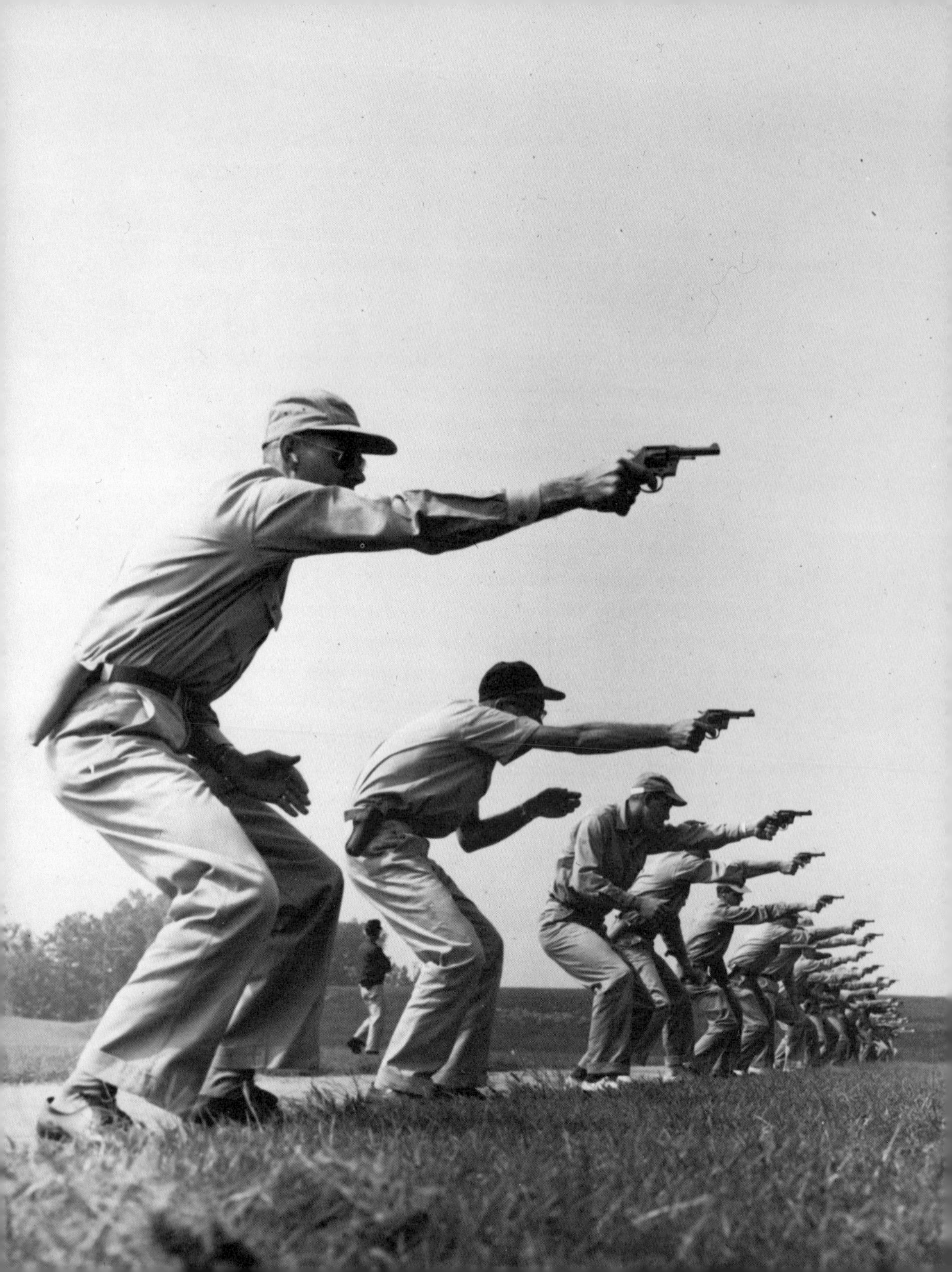

taught never to fire a gun unless the life of the Agent, or the life of another, is in danger. Then, when the Agent shoots, he or she shoots to kill.

During the last weeks of the course, much of the recruit's time is spent solving practical problems. A small group of recruits, for example, is brought to a room that looks like a bank office just after a robbery. The members of the group must work together to solve the crime. They must look for pieces of evidence, fingerprints, and other clues to help identify the criminal.

Other practical problems are to take part in a make-believe gunfight, to plan an investigation based on a ransom note from a kidnaper, to go with a team of recruits to free hostages being held by an armed airplane hijacker.

In each case, an experienced Agent watches as the recruits solve the problem. Then the Agent discusses their actions with them. What things did they do well? What mistakes did they make? This type of training helps the Agents-to-be to work together as a team. The recruits find out that it is more important to work with others than to become a lone hero.

There are frequent tests during the fifteen-week period. The classroom passing grade is 85 percent. A recruit who cannot keep up with the work is dropped. About one of every twenty-five recruits either fails or drops out of the Academy.

At the end of the training period, the recruit becomes a Special Agent. He or she is assigned to an FBI office. For several days, the new Agent goes out on cases with an experienced Agent. The

At the Academy, Special Agents practice on the shooting range.

Clerks, typists and secretaries at work in the Personnel Records section at FBI Headquarters.

new Agent learns by watching and, as each day passes, is given more and more responsibility. Then, finally, he or she starts to investigate cases without help. But squad leaders and supervisors continue to work closely with the Agent in these investigations.

For every two Special Agents in the bureau, there are about three clerical or technical workers. An applicant for a clerical job must be a citizen of the United States, a high school graduate, at least sixteen years of age, of good character, in good physical condition, and able to pass a spelling test. Clerical workers do not need prior experience. They receive on-the-job training. They help the Agents file reports, check records, deliver messages, answer the telephone, and in many other ways.

Clerks already working for the bureau may become fingerprint examiners. When there is an opening for an examiner, they can apply for the position. If they show an ability for this type of work, they are trained for this higher-paying job.

A fingerprint examiner classifies the patterns of new fingerprints that arrive from FBI offices and from police stations all over the country. They match up the new fingerprints with fingerprints already in the FBI file to identify suspects.

Typists and stenographers are also clerical workers. They earn more than clerks. But they must pass a test to be hired. Typists must be able to type forty words per minute. Stenographers or secretaries must be able to take eighty words per minute in shorthand.

People with special skills that are needed by the FBI are hired for the technical positions. Applicants who know three or more languages very well are hired as translators. Photographers and radio and communications experts are hired for their technical abilities. Men and women with college degrees in chemistry, biology, physics, or computer science find positions in the laboratories or headquarters of the FBI.

The men and women who work for the FBI have many chances for advancement. Every year a number of clerks earn their college degrees while working for the FBI. Some of them then go on to become Special Agents. The outstanding Special Agents are chosen for the higher positions in the bureau. All leadership positions are filled by promoting people already in the FBI. As a clerk, technical worker, or Special Agent, a career with the FBI is satisfying and purposeful.

SPECIAL AGENTS AT WORK

It was a little before eight o'clock in the morning. The Special Agents arriving at the Portland, Oregon, FBI Field Office picked up their mail and messages. They went into the squad room of the bank robbery and fugitive squad. Soon the room was noisy and crowded with chatting Agents.

In a little while, the Agents got to work. They took out the folders on their cases from the big, round rotary file cabinet in the corner of the room. Some removed their jackets, took their guns out of their holsters, and placed them in the desk drawers. Several plugged in their walkie-talkie radios to recharge the batteries.

The Agents added pages of new information to the folders. They wrote up reports of interviews they had completed. They reviewed their cases to see what progress had been made. They checked over their notes, and mapped out their activities for the day.

By nine o'clock, the Agents began to leave the squad room. Down in the garage, they entered unmarked FBI cars. Off they drove, two to a car, to follow up leads and question witnesses, suspects, and victims on cases that they had under investigation. "Street work," as they call it, takes up most of an Agent's time.

Two Agents were out on their street work when a message

came over the car radio: "Robbery at the Halsey Branch of the Citizens Valley Bank." The local police had already been called. But since it was a bank robbery, it was also a case for the FBI.

The two Agents knew just what they had to do. The driver turned the car around and sped toward the bank office. There they joined the Halsey police who were already on the scene. Together with the police, they questioned the tellers and the bank manager. They jotted down all the details of the robbery that the people who worked in the bank and the customers could recall.

Soon they had gathered the following story: Two men wearing masks and red wigs had burst through the bank's main door with drawn guns, and had announced a holdup. They had emptied all the money from the tellers' drawers into bags, and had scooped up all the money from the vault. Then they had forced everyone into the vault. The two men fled through the front door with nearly $17,000 in cash, including $340 in new half-dollars.

One of the FBI Agents searched the bank office very carefully. He photographed the inside of the bank from the front door, from the tellers' windows, from the vault, and from other angles, too. He traced the robbers' movements, and made pencil drawings of their positions during the holdup. He dusted the counters and drawers for fingerprints, and went over the floor for any item that might have been dropped during the robbery.

His partner, meanwhile, went outside to look for witnesses to the getaway. Several people had noticed a car parked outside the bank at the time of the robbery. They reported that two men were seated in the car. Some others had seen the car speed away from the scene. All the witnesses agreed that the car was small, red, and about ten years old.

The search, the questioning, and the fingerprints gave scant

Special Agents must be well versed in law and are expected to keep up-to-date on legal procedures.

information. The biggest lead was the color and model of the getaway car.

The FBI Agents stayed on the case now, day after day, trying to develop new leads based on the car. They went to used-car lots to see if a small, old red car had recently been sold. They visited gasoline stations, repair shops, car auctions, dumps — wherever and whoever might tell them something about the car and the men who had used the car in the robbery.

No one knew anything about the car for which the FBI Agents were searching. The Agents were no closer to solving the robbery. Since they had several other active cases, they began spending more time on those investigations. They spent less time on the Halsey case.

The first real break in the Halsey robbery came many weeks later. A farmer reported finding an abandoned, old red car in a field about three miles outside of Halsey. Now the FBI Agents followed this lead. They made frequent visits to the area. They uncovered a few people who did remember seeing the car, with two men in it. They described the men to the two FBI Agents. But again the Agents came to a dead end. None of the witnesses could identify the two men.

While the Agents were pursuing these leads, though, there were two other bank robberies in towns near Halsey. Both had been robbed by two armed men wearing masks and red wigs. After each of these robberies, the getaway car was found abandoned not far from the scene of the crime. Since the *modus operandi*, or "method of operation," of all three robberies was so similar, the Agents guessed that they were done by the same men.

The two Agents went over the case carefully in their office. They reviewed the folder which was kept in the file. They talked things over with their boss, the Special Agent in Charge of the Portland Field Office. The robbers now had plenty of cash. They abandoned their cars after each job. The Agents had a description of the two men. They decided on a new approach to the case: Call on all the car dealers in the area. Get the name of anyone who had recently bought a car for cash. Follow up each lead. Investigate until someone is found with lots of spare cash, but no explanation of where it came from.

The new line of investigation went on for many days. Time after time, the Agents found that the used cars had been bought by honest citizens with legal money. But then, the investigation led to a suspicious individual. This individual matched the description of one of the men seen at the bank robbery.

The Agents knew that they were getting close. Dozens more people were interviewed. Hundreds more questions were asked. They learned that within a few days the man had bought a pick-up truck, a station wagon, and a houseful of furniture. Though he was unemployed, he had paid for everything in cash. His trail led to another man, also unemployed, who had agreed to pay over $4,000 in cash for a car at about the same time.

The pace of the investigation quickened. The Agents discovered that the two men were friends. One of them had been seen in Halsey just before the robbery at the Citizens Valley Bank. The other one was observed spending shiny new half-dollars in a local bar.

By now, the Agents were convinced that they had enough evidence of the guilt of the two suspects. They prepared the necessary papers, and brought them to the United States Attorney in Portland, Oregon. The Attorney studied the evidence in the case. He gave approval for arrest warrants to be obtained. The charge

Science in the FBI Lab plays an invaluable role in the apprehension of criminals.

— conspiracy to commit robbery against banks insured by the federal government.

That same day, one of the men was stopped by a local police officer while driving his car. FBI Agents examined the car thoroughly. On the car floor were two guns and two full-face masks. Later that night, the second man was picked up at his home. Although the Agents had their guns with them while making the arrests, neither man offered any resistance.

After the arrests, the FBI Agents interviewed the men. Both confessed to having taken part in the robberies. They admitted the purchases of the cars. At their trial, they were found guilty of robbery, and sentenced to long terms in prison.

By this time, the Agents were already at work on other cases. They follow the same procedure in all criminal cases: First, search the crime scene for clues that might help them to solve the case. Then, develop leads and interview to collect more evidence. Finally, present the evidence to a United States Attorney.

Criminals almost always leave something behind at the scene of a crime. It is the Agent's job to find it. A hat, a fingerprint, a bit of dirt from a shoe, a strand of hair, a thread of clothing, can help to find the criminal.

Special Agents sometimes put suspects under constant watch. If federal laws permit them to do so, the Special Agent may get permission from court to tap the suspect's phone or to use other listening devices. Interviews with neighbors, storekeepers, friends, relatives, and fellow workers are usually conducted in a friendly way. Agents do all they can to encourage witnesses and others to report information concerning criminal activities.

Once a federal warrant has been issued for the arrest of a suspect, FBI Agents carefully plan the arrest. Often, they surprise the suspect. Also, enough Agents are present so that the arrest is made without fighting and without gunfire.

Bank robberies and fugitives who are fleeing arrest are cases handled by one squad in the Field Office. Other squads handle the other crimes that come under the jurisdiction of the FBI.

A general investigative squad looks into crimes in which goods are taken across state lines, crimes that take place on government land or in government buildings, or crimes that involve the stealing of government property. A squad works on cases of organized crime such as gambling, loan-sharking, prostitution, and other rackets.

There are other squads that handle cases of bombing and terrorism, of radical groups that are believed to be working against the United States government, and espionage investigations. (In 1976, Director Kelley ordered a sharp reduction in the number of security investigations.)

And there is the applicant squad that searches the backgrounds of people who are applying for certain staff jobs in the White House, the Department of Justice, Congress, and certain other government agencies. The FBI conducts hundreds of applicant investigations a year. They gather and report the information, but do not determine the suitability for employment of the people they investigate.

A few of the Special Agents in each Field Office are also members of the SWAT (Special Weapons and Tactics) team. SWAT team members are experts in the use of firearms. They are in top physical condition. The team is brought together to handle highly dangerous situations.

A SWAT team may go into action to arrest one of the Top Ten Wanted Criminals, to rescue hostages, in kidnaping or hijacking cases, or to capture fugitives in wilderness areas. The SWAT team is trained to use special equipment — automatic rifles, tear gas, gas masks, ropes for climbing mountains or entering the upper windows of buildings, and so on. The SWAT team is always ready, in top-flight condition, to do what is needed, whenever or wherever.

The job of a Special Agent is varied, and fascinating. No two cases are ever exactly the same. Every case is a new challenge, a new contest. It is a contest between the Agent and the criminal. If the criminal gets away with the crime, the Agent has lost the contest. If the Agent finds the evidence and the criminal is captured, the Agent has won.

FBI Special Agents are skillful and proud men and women. They win many more times than they lose.

THE FBI LAB

EXPLOSIVES

A government scientist working in an eastern city recently received a package in the mail. As he was opening the box on his dining room table, it exploded. The young man was killed.

Explosives experts from the FBI were sent to the scene. They gathered together the far-flung fragments of the package. They sifted through the debris. They sorted and labeled each item of interest and placed it in a jar or envelope. All the evidence was then sent to the FBI Laboratory for tests.

The FBI Laboratory, in the FBI Headquarters in Washington, D.C., is the largest crime lab in the world. About four hundred scientists, called examiners, work there. Among them are some of the world's leading experts in the different branches of science that are used to solve crimes.

The evidence from the bombing was given to examiners in the explosives unit of the Laboratory. Each examiner has a thorough knowledge of homemade bombs. Each one knows all the types of explosives that are used, and the many methods used to set off the blast. For days, they peered at the material through high-powered microscopes. They performed tests to discover the exact chemicals used in the explosive.

Finally, they wrote out their report: The explosive in the package was dynamite. The dynamite had been placed in a black imitation leather case. The case was tied with a piece of Venetian blind cord, and packed in a cardboard shipping container.

The cord was attached to wires that ran to a battery and to a switch. When the scientist lifted the black case out of the cardboard box, the cord tightened and pulled the switch closed. The closed switch completed the electrical circuit, and exploded the dynamite.

Other FBI Agents, meanwhile, learned that the scientist's former girl friend was involved with a married man in California. This man was jealous of the scientist. He was afraid that the girl might leave him and return to her former boyfriend.

With the permission of the man's wife, FBI Agents in California searched the house. They found two items of interest: a pair of pliers and a length of Venetian blind cord. They sent these items to the FBI Lab.

The examiners looked at the evidence through a microscope. They found that some nicks on the pliers matched nicks found on the wires that were attached to the battery. It was clear that the pliers had been used to join the wires in the bomb package. Furthermore, the Venetian blind cord found in California matched exactly the tiny bits of cord recovered from the bomb debris.

Shortly thereafter, the California man's body was found in a pond near his home. He was an apparent suicide.

The explosives unit is just one part of the FBI Lab. There are over a dozen other units. Each one specializes in one type of police science. As each case comes into the Lab, it is sent to the unit that is best able to use science to solve that case.

FIREARMS

One day, a package containing a gun, a bullet, and a woman's blouse arrived at the FBI Lab from Wyoming. The gun had been found near the body of the dead woman. The bullet had been recovered from her body. And she had been wearing the blouse at the time of the shooting. The question the examiners had to answer was: murder or suicide?

Experts in the firearms unit of the Lab examined the gun, and noted the exact make and model of the weapon. They loaded the gun with a bullet, and fired it into a large tank of water. They took the bullet from the water and the bullet from Wyoming, and placed them side by side under a microscope. Both bullets showed exactly the same tiny scratches. The identical marks showed that both bullets were fired from the same gun. The scientists, therefore, positively identified the gun as the weapon used in the crime. The gun had belonged to the dead woman.

The blouse was examined for traces of gunpowder or burn marks. There were none. The absence of such marks meant that the gun had been fired from a distance greater than thirty-six inches. This ruled out the possibility that the woman had shot herself. This was a case of murder, not suicide.

This expert is examining a weapon for possible addition to the FBI's extensive collection of firearms.

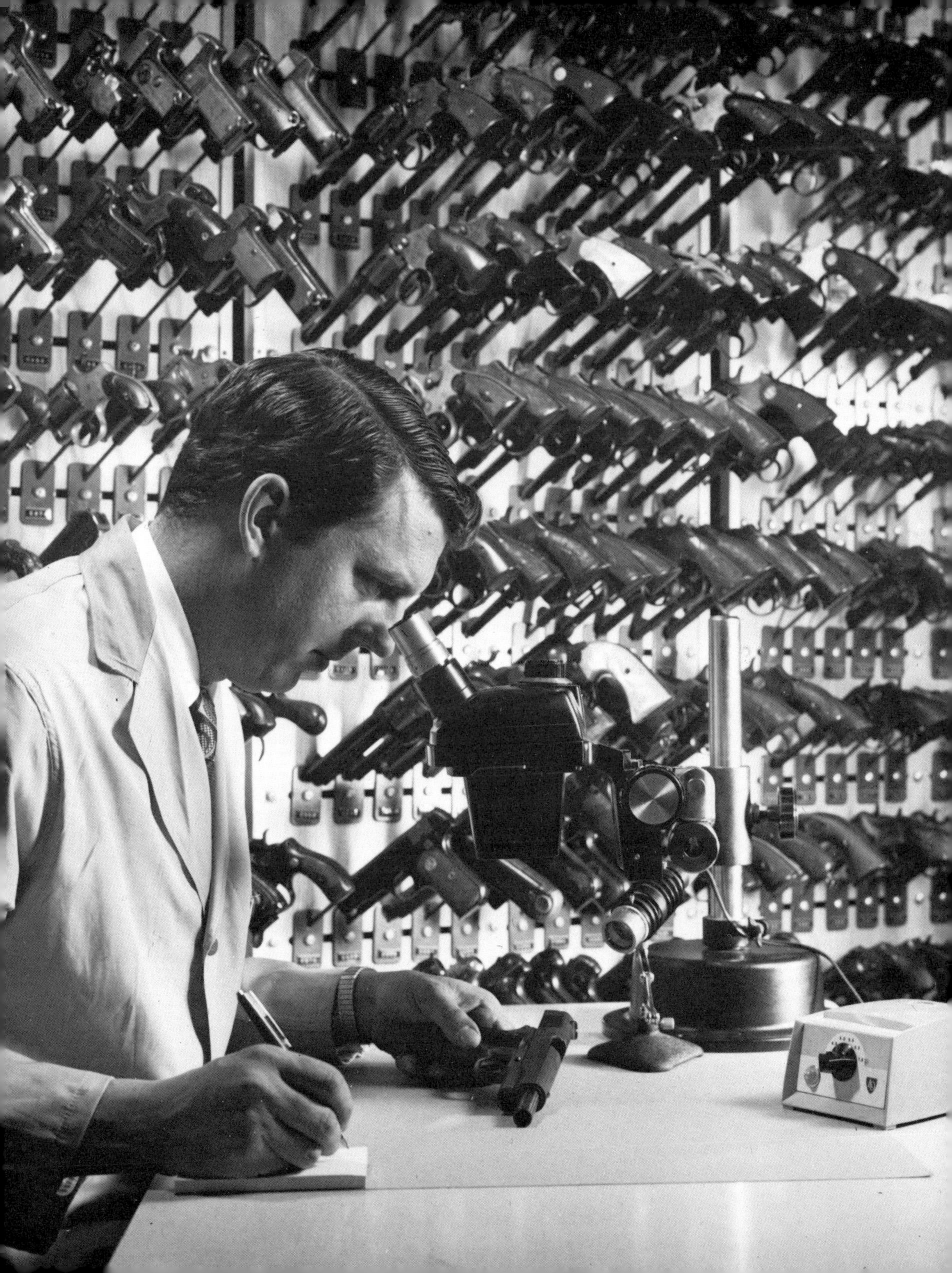

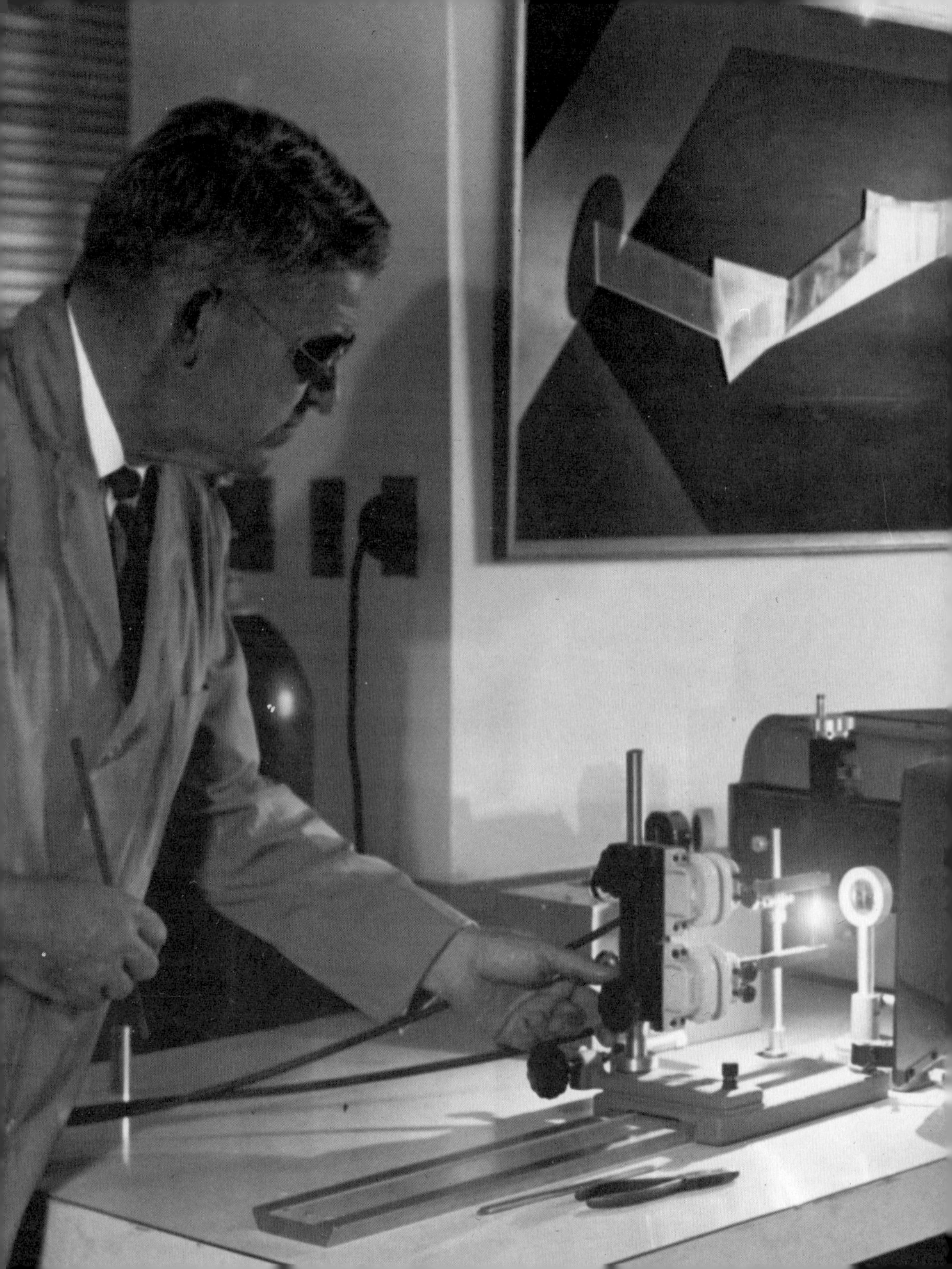

The woman's boyfriend was brought in as a suspect. On the basis of the Lab reports, he was indicted for first degree murder. He pleaded innocent. Just before the trial, though, he changed his plea to guilty of manslaughter. He told how he had shot his girl friend with her own gun after they had quarreled. The boyfriend was sentenced to serve from eighteen to twenty years for manslaughter.

INSTRUMENT ANALYSIS

In another FBI Lab case, a ten-year-old girl was killed by a hit-and-run driver. But no one saw the accident occur.

The local police sent the victim's clothing to the instrument analysis unit of the Lab. The examiners in this unit are expert in using instruments to find evidence that is not easily found by other means. They can identify and compare many different kinds of evidence, such as paints, plastics, metal, glass, and rubber.

Among the threads of the girl's jacket, an examiner found a tiny speck of paint, no larger than the dot at the end of this sentence. He examined the tiny paint chip under a very powerful microscope. He saw that the hit-and-run vehicle was painted with a gold metallic acrylic paint.

The examiner's next step was to consult the FBI Lab's Automotive Paint File. Here are kept samples of all the paints used on autos in the United States. By matching the chip of paint to a sam-

This instrument, called an emission spectrograph, can analyse the chemical composition of evidence.

ple in the collection, the examiner found out the year and model of the hit-and-run car.

With these clues, the police located a suspect who lived in the same neighborhood as the victim. The bent hood of his car was delivered to the FBI Lab.

Examiners found that the paint chip from the girl's clothing matched exactly the paint of the hood. On the hood, too, they noticed some tiny threads. By instrument analysis, the Laboratory scientists discovered that the threads on the hood were the same as the threads of the child's jacket.

This Laboratory evidence was used to indict the suspect. The FBI experts later testified at the trial, and the neighbor was found guilty.

BLOOD

In Indiana, a suspect was arrested for having illegally killed several Canada geese. He denied the charge. A United States game warden investigating the matter found a blood-stained cardboard box in the suspect's house. He believed that the suspect had used the box to carry the quarry home. The suspect claimed that the stains came from a cut on his hand.

The warden sent a piece of the bloodied cardboard box to the FBI Lab. He wanted the examiners to find out whether the blood was from a bird or from a human being.

In the Laboratory, the examiners scraped off little specks of dried blood from the cardboard. They performed several different chemical tests on each sample. In every case, the results were the same. The blood was positively human blood. There was no blood from any type of bird or fowl.

On the basis of the FBI Lab report, the suspect was cleared.

An FBI laboratory expert examines evidence for the presence of blood.

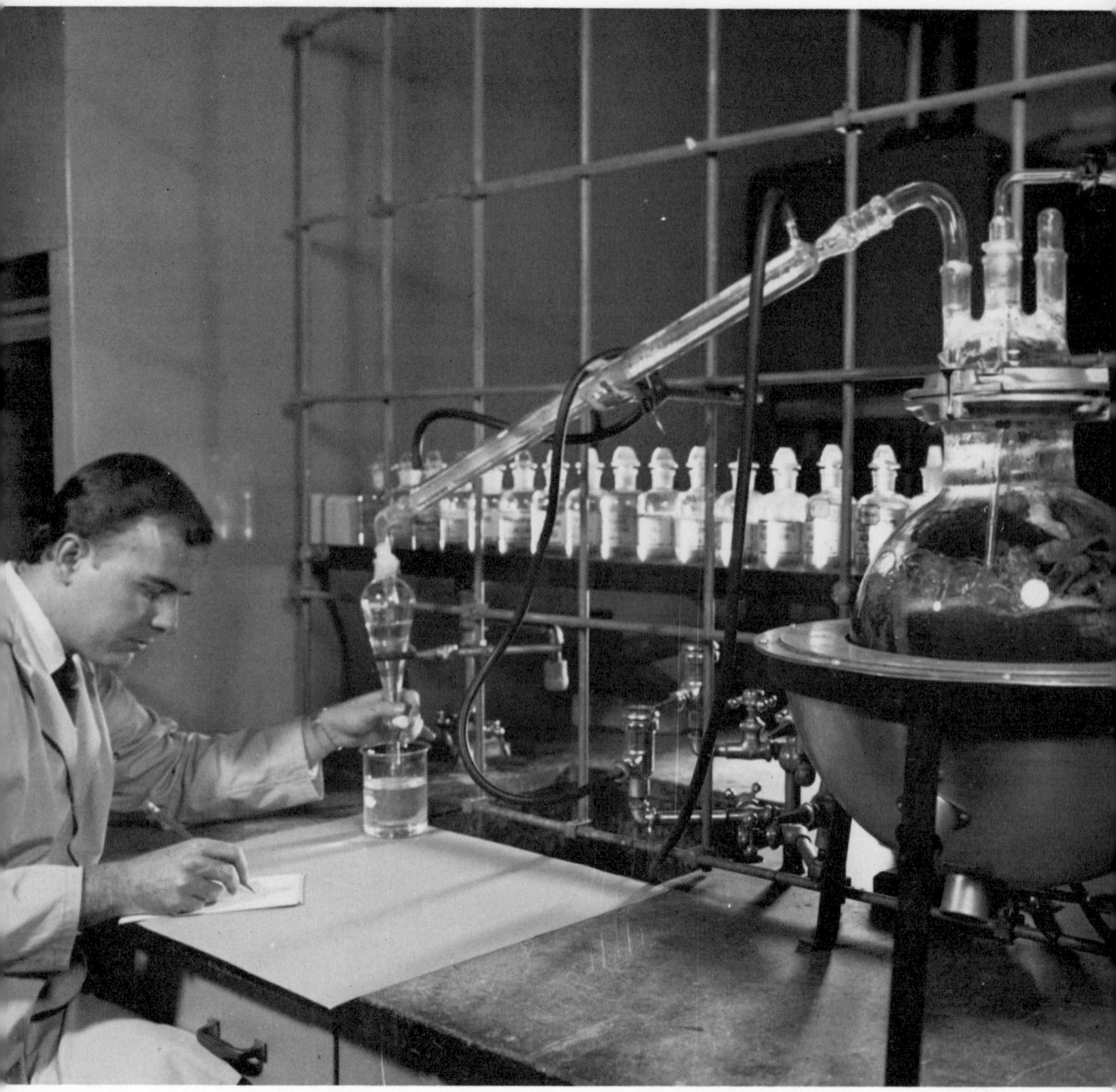

CHEMISTRY

In another state, a man tried to rob a bank using a water pistol loaded with some unknown liquid as the weapon. The robbery was foiled when a frightened bank teller began to scream, and the criminal ran from the bank. Bank officials chased him. Out on the street, the would-be robber turned and "shot" the officials.

The police later captured the robber, and recovered the water pistol. It still contained some of the liquid. They sent it to the FBI Lab to identify the contents. FBI chemists put the liquid through a whole series of tests. They used many different complicated methods and advanced instruments to find out what was in the liquid.

Each test narrowed down the number of possible substances in the water pistol. Finally, it came down to a single substance — a solution of ammonia. Ammonia is a powerful, dangerous solution. It can easily damage the eyes and cause blindness.

The water pistol, therefore, was not a toy. It was a dangerous weapon. And the defendant was found guilty of attempted bank robbery with a dangerous weapon.

SHOE AND TIRE IMPRESSIONS

A jewelry store in the South was burglarized one night. The thief broke in through a back window, forced open the safe, and made off with jewelry valued at $20,000.

In this FBI Chemistry Lab,
an arson case is being investigated.

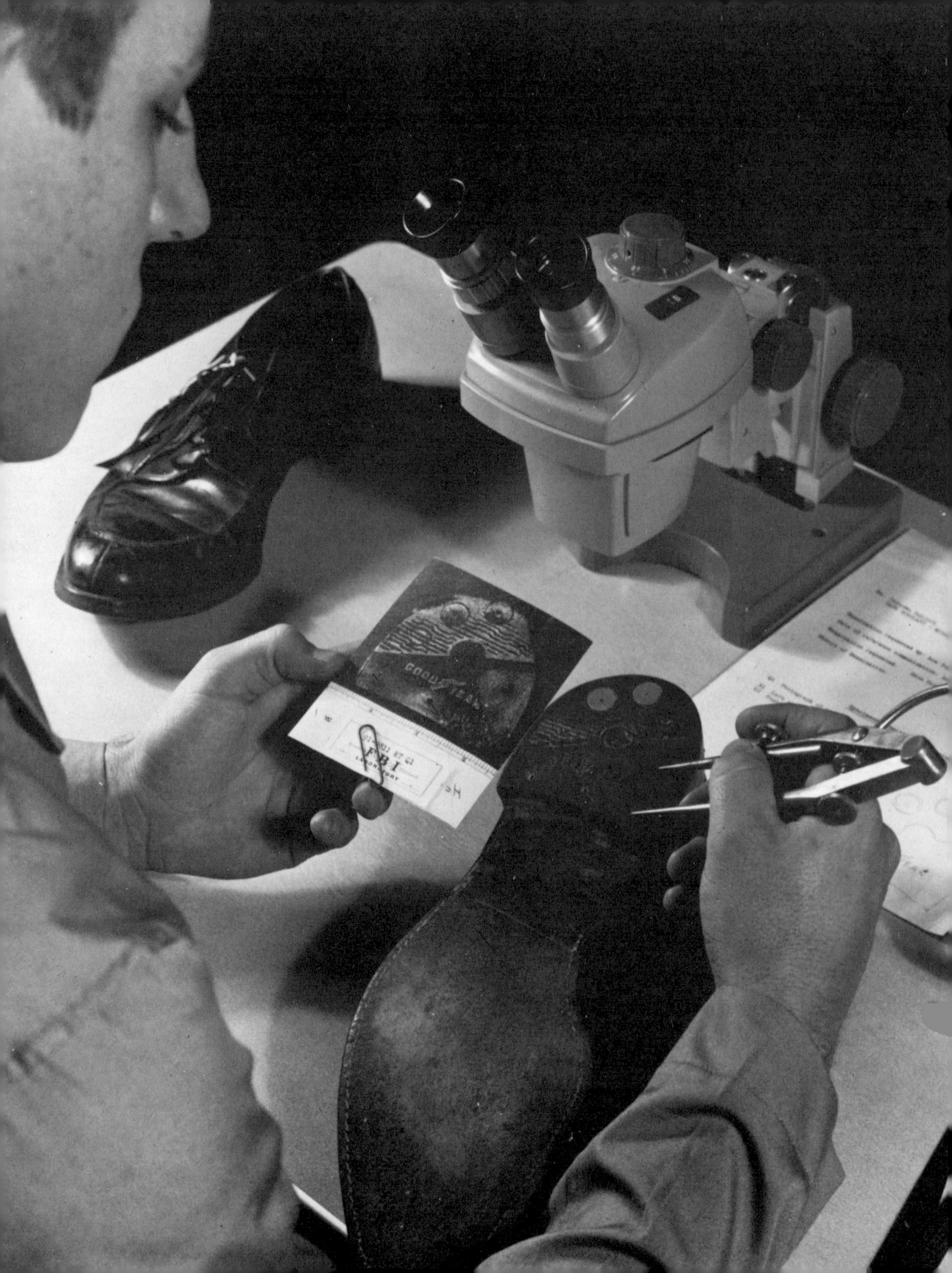
F B I

Left: heel prints of a suspect's shoes are compared with a photograph taken from the scene of a crime. Above: an actual tire is compared with a plaster cast to determine whether the suspect's car was involved in a crime.

In the parking lot behind the store, the local police found some fresh shoe prints and tire marks. They made plaster casts of these marks, and sent them to the FBI Lab for examination.

Laboratory experts searched through the FBI's Shoe Print File and the Tire Tread File. They were able to identify the make and size of both the shoe and tire impressions. They sent the results of their examinations back to the local police.

Sometime later, the police picked up a suspect in another jewelry store burglary. The tires on his car and the heels of his shoes appeared to match the tire marks and heel prints that were found at the scene of the burglary. His tires and shoes were sent to the FBI Lab to be compared with the casts from the earlier burglary.

The Laboratory experts reported that the tires on the suspect's car had made the impressions found near the crime scene. And the heels on the suspect's shoes had made the heel prints found outside the jewelry store.

When he was told of the FBI report, the suspect pleaded guilty, and was convicted of the jewelry store burglary.

DOCUMENT

The FBI Agents working on a kidnaping case on Long Island, New York, had only one clue — a handwritten ransom note. Handwriting experts at the FBI Lab were given the job of identifying the kidnaper from this one piece of evidence.

This document expert is hoping to determine if these two documents were signed by the same hand.

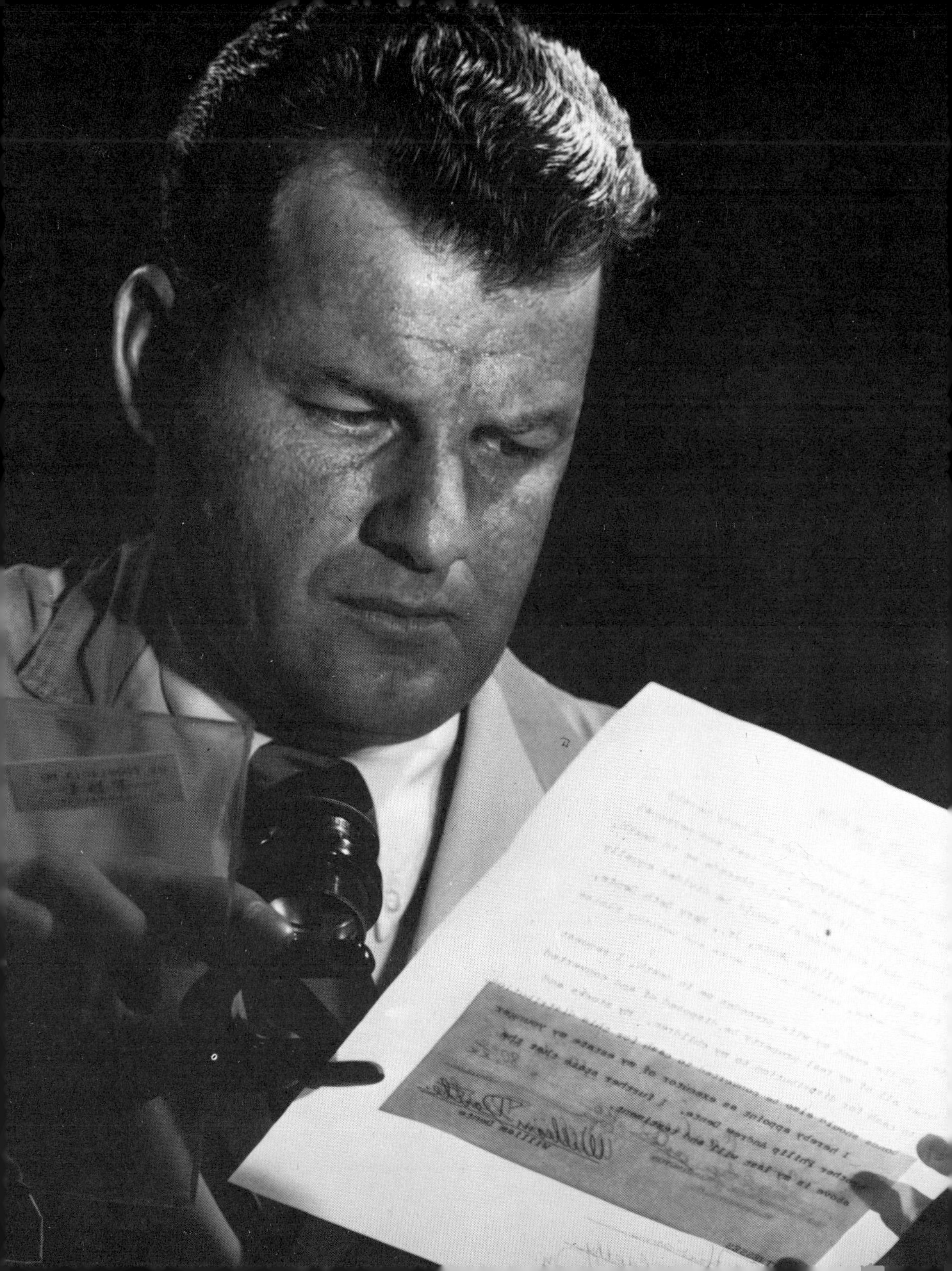

They began by going through the FBI's gigantic file of handwriting samples of known criminals. Then, with the help of agents from the New York Field Office, they went through handwriting samples in files of federal, state, and local agencies in the area.

The experts compared every similar sample in each of the files with the written note. They looked at the angle and the spacing of the letters, and the shape of the individual letters. Finally, after examining nearly two million samples, they found one that matched the handwriting on the note.

The suspect was picked up and brought in for questioning. He confessed to the kidnaping. He said that he needed the ransom money to pay off his debts. He led officers to the place where he had abandoned his victim to die.

Handwriting experts from the FBI Laboratory testified at the trial. The suspect was convicted, and sentenced to death for the kidnaping and murder.

Every year, the scientists in the FBI Lab do nearly five hundred thousand examinations. The evidence may be as small as a drop of blood or a snip of hair. It may be as large as the bent hood of an automobile or a partly burned wooden door. In each case, the Lab's examiners use all of their skills and all of the modern instruments and methods of the FBI Lab to solve the crime through science.

IDENTIFICATION DIVISION

FINGERPRINTS

Two policemen in Los Angeles received a call on their car radio to pick up a noisy drunk outside a downtown bar. They brought him to the station house, and booked him for disorderly conduct. They put him in a cell to sleep off his drunkenness.

As a routine matter, the police took his fingerprints. They spread some printer's ink on a slab of glass, and then pressed the man's fingers into the ink. Then they pressed each finger in turn onto ten spaces of an eight-inch square card. The raised ridges on his fingertips left clear patterns on the fingerprint card.

A copy of his fingerprints was sent electronically to the Identification Division of the FBI in Washington, D.C. The Identification Division has the largest collection of fingerprints in the world. More than 164 million sets of fingerprints are on file. Every day about 22,000 more are received. Every day, also, several hundred cards are removed. They include those on people who have died, who have reached a certain age, or who have been accused of minor crimes.

Workers in the Identification Division are on duty twenty-four hours a day. As soon as the prints arrived from Los Angeles, a technician took the name from the fingerprint card and went to the card index. Here, on millions of three-by-five-inch cards, are listed the names of all people with criminal records. A check through the cards did not turn up any information on the drunk in Los Angeles. Possibly the arrested man had given the police a false name.

Now another technician took the fingerprint card to classify the fingerprints according to the loops, arches, and whorls in the pattern. Using the classification code, the technician was then able to find twenty cards in the fingerprint file that fell into the same general classification.

The technician went over each set of prints. She made a careful study of the pattern for each finger. Finally, she came across an identical set of prints. She wrote the word "ident" on the fingerprint card. From the file card she learned that the man had, indeed, given the Los Angeles police a false name. His fingerprints, though, identified him as a fugitive who was wanted in Toledo, Ohio, on a charge of armed robbery and car theft. The fingerprint technician gave this information to the FBI communications office to be sent to the Los Angeles police.

Within an hour, the Los Angeles police received the identification information from FBI Headquarters. The drunk was not released the next day. Instead, he was held and turned over to the Toledo police. He stood trial for his past crimes, was convicted, and sentenced to jail.

Every year, the FBI Identification Division receives over five million requests for information. Every day, there are over one thousand criminals who are identified through the FBI's card index and fingerprint file.

More than half of all the fingerprint cards on file, about ninety million, are of noncriminals. They are civil records; fingerprints of members of the armed forces, government workers, aliens living in the United States, and so on. This makes the Iden-

Training class for FBI fingerprint technicians.

tification Division useful in many noncriminal matters. Over and over again, the Division is called to help locate missing persons, or to identify victims of amnesia (a loss of memory).

The Disaster Squad is a group of specially trained fingerprint technicians within the Identification Division. They are asked to identify victims of catastrophes where fingerprints might be the only means of identification. A plane crash, a bad fire, an earthquake, or a flood are situations that need their special skills to obtain fingerprints from the victims. The Disaster Squad is only brought together a few times a year — but for the families of those lost in the disaster, and the authorities, they perform a most valuable service.

Fingerprints are a positive means of identification. Names, signatures, personal appearances, and other characteristics can be changed. But fingerprints stay with a person from before birth until after death. Of all the millions of fingerprints the FBI technicians have classified, they have never found two prints that are exactly alike. Even identical twins, who are the same in every other way, have different fingerprints.

Fingerprints are the chief means of identification used by law enforcement agencies. In recent years, the efficiency and speed of classifying and locating fingerprints in a file have been much improved. In the near future, the FBI will begin to use an automatic fingerprint reader, called FINDER. The name is made up of the first three letters of fingerprint, and the last three letters of reader. As these amazing instruments are perfected, they will be able to classify fingerprints and search through the files for a match in just seconds. Someday, the entire fingerprint operation may be completely automated. This will free up to two thousand technicians and clerks for other work in the bureau. And it will save the government about $19 million a year.

NATIONAL CRIME INFORMATION CENTER

Two Michigan state troopers were cruising along the highway when a car whizzed by. It was traveling about seventy-five miles an hour. The trooper who was driving stepped on the gas to overtake the speeder. At the same time, his partner bent over the computer terminal under the dashboard. The device is linked to the computer of the National Crime Information Center (NCIC), which is located in the FBI Headquarters in Washington, D.C. On the small, typewriterlike machine, he punched in various code numbers. He also inserted the license plate number of the speeding car.

The NCIC is a central index of information on wanted persons, criminal histories, and stolen property. The memory of the NCIC computer contains about 6½ million separate records. This information is available, within minutes, to any police agency with a computer terminal that is linked, directly or indirectly, to the NCIC computer.

The Michigan troopers managed to overtake the speeding car. They brought it to a halt along the side of the road. By this time, they had received the report from the NCIC on their computer terminal. A car with that license number had been used by two armed men in the robbery of a stock broker's office in North Carolina two days earlier. During the getaway a policeman was shot and killed.

The troopers now realized that these men might be a pair of desperate criminals. They were likely to be armed and dangerous. They proceeded with great caution. One officer approached the stopped car with drawn gun, while the other one covered him from the protection of the police car.

The desperadoes surrendered without a struggle. They were

Workers in the FBI National Crime Information Center control room.

taken to the police station in handcuffs. In time, they were returned to North Carolina to stand trial for murder.

The NCIC computer is available to law enforcement agencies twenty-four hours a day. It receives an average of more than two requests for information every second. And it scores about one thousand "hits" every day. It is a hit when a wanted fugitive is captured because of information from the NCIC. It is also a hit when stolen property is recovered and returned to its rightful owner.

TEN MOST WANTED FUGITIVES

C.D.B.; wanted for the bombing of four electric transmission towers in Colorado. He was identified through fingerprints after he was taken into custody by the police in Rhode Island.

S.E.S.; sought for bank robbery and murder. She was picked up by a Philadelphia, Pennsylvania, police officer, who recognized her from an FBI poster.

R.B.L.; wanted for transporting a stolen motor vehicle across state lines and bank robbery. He was traced by FBI Agents to a trailer park in Florida. Although there were several weapons in his trailer, he did not resist arrest.

W.L.H.; wanted fugitive who escaped from a Kentucky prison where he was serving a life sentence for murder. FBI Agents caught him after a high-speed auto chase in Illinois.

J.W.S.; wanted bank robber who escaped from prison where he was serving a sentence for bank robbery. He was arrested by police in the Washington, D.C., suburbs on a tip that he was hiding in the trunk of an automobile.

These five criminals were among seven captured in one year recently after being listed among the Ten Most Wanted Fugitives.

The Top Ten program, as it is called, was started by the FBI in 1950. The bureau prints posters that include pictures, descriptions, and accounts of the crimes of the ten most-wanted criminals in the country. These men and women are considered to be the most violent and dangerous of all the criminals being sought by the FBI. Top Ten notices are hung in post offices, police stations, and in public buildings. Sometimes newspapers or television stations also carry stories on the Top Ten.

From the start of the Top Ten program, through August 1976, 344 fugitives have been listed. Of these, 319 have been captured. It is, of course, a changing list. After a criminal is caught, another one is added.

Many of the Top Ten criminals were captured because of the wide publicity given to the program. Often the public helped by providing information to FBI Agents or police officers.

Look for the Ten Most Wanted Fugitives posters in this book, or at your post office or police station. Then keep an eye out for the men and women whose pictures you have seen. If you spot one of them, or think you do, here is what the FBI wants you to do: Give the criminal no sign of recognition. Make no attempt to be a hero or heroine. Notice as many details as possible. Remember what he or she is wearing; the license number if in a car. Observe what the suspect is doing and where he or she seems to be heading. Look to see if the suspect is alone or with someone else. Then, get to a telephone quickly and call the nearest FBI office. You will find the number on the first page of most telephone directories.

The FBI needs the help of the public in capturing the Top Ten, and in solving its other cases as well. With the cooperation of all its citizens, the United States will become safer and more free of crime.

TEN MOST-WANTED CRIMINALS

INTERSTATE FLIGHT – MURDER; THEFT OF GOVERNMENT PROPERTY; BANK ROBBERY

WANTED BY FBI
KATHERINE ANN POWER

Entered NCIC
I.O. 4402
10-2-70
(Rev. 8-2-73)

FBI No. 545,574 H

ALIAS: Helen

NO FINGERPRINTS AVAILABLE

Photograph taken 1969 — Photograph taken 1970 — Date photograph taken unknown

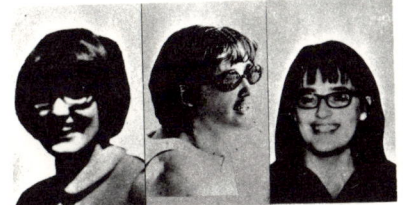

DESCRIPTION
- AGE: 24, born January 25, 1949, Denver, Colorado
- HEIGHT: 5'
- WEIGHT: 145 to 150 pounds
- BUILD: stocky
- HAIR: light brown, may be dyed black
- EYES: hazel
- COMPLEXION: medium
- RACE: white
- NATIONALITY: American
- SCARS AND MARKS: pockmark on left cheek, appendectomy scar, large scar on abdomen
- SOCIAL SECURITY NUMBER USED: 522-74-2089

CAUTION
POWER MAY BE ACCOMPANIED BY SUSAN EDITH SAXE, FBI IDENTIFICATION ORDER 4403. BOTH MAY BE ARMED AND SHOULD BE CONSIDERED VERY DANGEROUS.

Federal warrants were issued on September 24, 1970, at Boston, Massachusetts, charging Power with unlawful interstate flight to avoid prosecution for murder (Title 18, U.S. Code, Section 1073); on September 25, 1970, with theft of Government property (Title 18, U.S. Code, Section 641); and on October 1, 1970, at Philadelphia, Pennsylvania, with bank robbery (Title 18, U.S. Code, Sections 2113a, b and d).

IF YOU HAVE INFORMATION CONCERNING THIS PERSON, PLEASE CONTACT YOUR LOCAL FBI OFFICE. TELEPHONE NUMBERS AND ADDRESSES OF ALL FBI OFFICES LISTED ON BACK.

C. M. Kelley

Identification Order 4402
October 2, 1970

INTERSTATE FLIGHT – MURDER

WANTED BY FBI
ROY ELLSWORTH SMITH

Entered NCIC
I.O. 4731
12-17-76

FBI No. 741,521 G

17 L 1 U 7
S 1 Ut

ALIASES: Roy Ellsworth Smith, Jr., Roy E. Smith

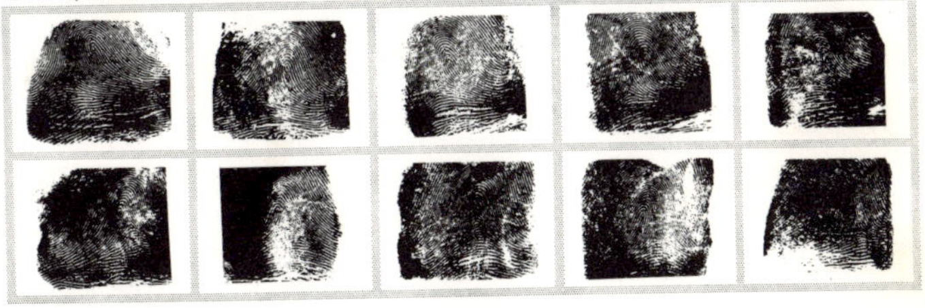

NCIC: 17130812070505TT0813

Photographs taken 1970 — Photograph taken 1975

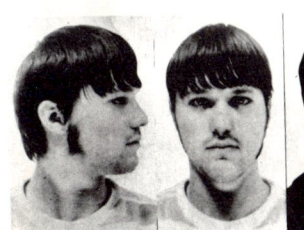

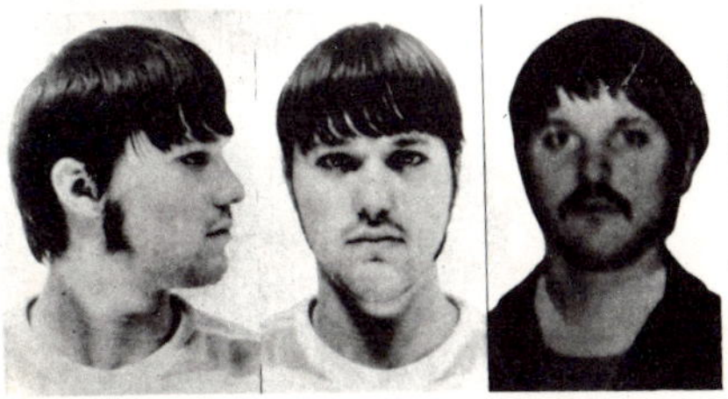

Roy Ellsworth Smith

DESCRIPTION
- AGE: 27, born November 30, 1949, Painesville, Ohio
- HEIGHT: 5'11" to 6'
- WEIGHT: 150 to 160 pounds
- BUILD: slender
- HAIR: brown
- EYES: blue
- COMPLEXION: medium
- RACE: white
- NATIONALITY: American
- OCCUPATIONS: clerk, custodian, dishwasher, handyman, plasterer's helper
- SCARS AND MARKS: scar on left shoulder, appendectomy scar
- REMARKS: may be wearing mustache and/or goatee, reportedly is a frequent user of alcohol.
- SOCIAL SECURITY NUMBER USED: 284-52-6808

CRIMINAL RECORD
Smith has been convicted of statutory rape.

CAUTION
SMITH, A REPORTED NARCOTICS USER WHO IS USUALLY ARMED WITH A SWITCH-BLADE-TYPE KNIFE AND HANDGUN, IS BEING SOUGHT IN CONNECTION WITH THE RUTHLESS MURDERS OF TWO CHILDREN WHO WERE REPEATEDLY BLUDGEONED WITH A HAMMER. HE SHOULD BE CONSIDERED ARMED AND DANGEROUS.

A Federal warrant was issued on May 13, 1976, at Cleveland, Ohio, charging Smith with unlawful interstate flight to avoid prosecution for the crime of murder (Title 18, U.S. Code, Section 1073).

IF YOU HAVE INFORMATION CONCERNING THIS PERSON, PLEASE CONTACT YOUR LOCAL FBI OFFICE. TELEPHONE NUMBERS AND ADDRESSES OF ALL FBI OFFICES LISTED ON BACK.

C. M. Kelley
Director
Federal Bureau of Investigation
Washington, D.C. 20535

Identification Order 4731
December 17, 1976

Entered NCIC
I. O. 4707
6-24-76

INTERSTATE FLIGHT - MURDER

WANTED BY FBI

LARRY GENE CAMPBELL

FBI No. 178,503 E

ALIASES: Harry Bailey, Earl Jerido, Earl Jerie, Rudolph Richardson

NCIC: 13TT07131214TT080813

13 M 1 T II 12 Ref: R T R
M 1 T II — T R R

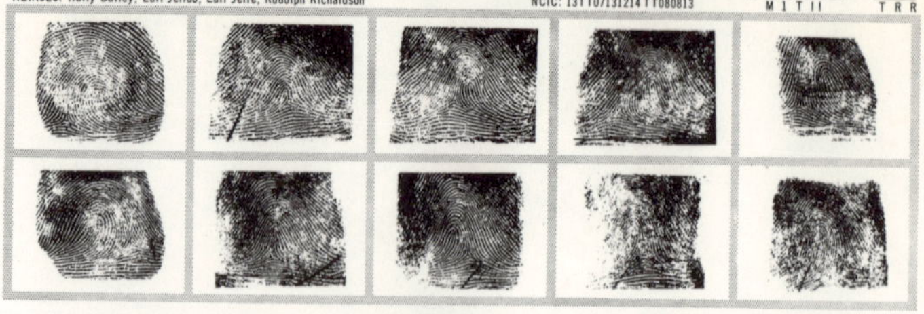

Photograph taken 1975 — Photograph taken 1976

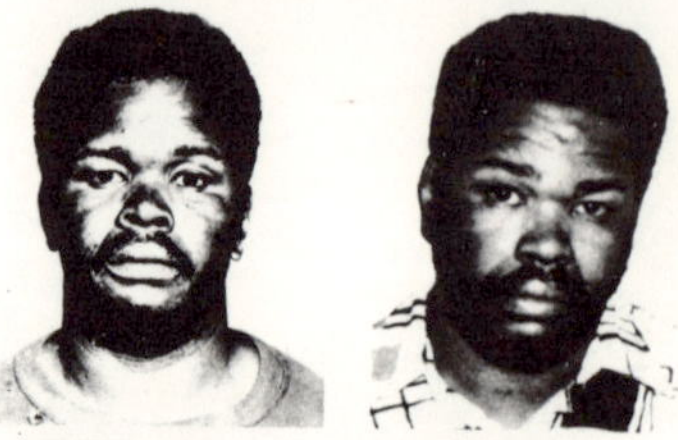

Larry G. Campbell

DESCRIPTION

AGE: 33, born August 12, 1942, Valdosta, Georgia (not supported by birth records)
HEIGHT: 5'10"
WEIGHT: 195 pounds
BUILD: stocky
HAIR: black
EYES: brown
COMPLEXION: dark
RACE: Negro
NATIONALITY: American
OCCUPATIONS: clerk, laborer, plumber, radio operator, steamfitter
SCARS AND MARKS: scars on both inner lower forearms
SOCIAL SECURITY NUMBER USED: 041-32-5154

CRIMINAL RECORD

Campbell has been convicted of burglary and possession of narcotics.

CAUTION

CAMPBELL, A REPORTED NARCOTICS USER, IS BEING SOUGHT FOR THE JUNE 8, 1976, BRUTAL STABBING AND STRANGULATION MURDERS OF TWO COLLEGE STUDENTS. HE SHOULD BE CONSIDERED ARMED AND EXTREMELY DANGEROUS.

A Federal warrant was issued on June 11, 1976, at Buffalo, New York, charging Campbell with unlawful interstate flight to avoid prosecution for the crime of murder (Title 18, U. S. Code, Section 1073).

IF YOU HAVE INFORMATION CONCERNING THIS PERSON, PLEASE CONTACT YOUR LOCAL FBI OFFICE. TELEPHONE NUMBERS AND ADDRESSES OF ALL FBI OFFICES LISTED ON BACK.

Identification Order 4707
June 24, 1976

Director
Federal Bureau of Investigation
Washington, D. C. 20535

Entered NCIC
I. O. 4693
3-3-76

INTERSTATE STOLEN PROPERTY; CONSPIRACY

WANTED BY FBI

JOSEPH MAURICE MC DONALD

FBI No. 863,391 B

ALIASES: Thomas Campbell, Joseph Maurice MacDonald, Joe McDonald, Joseph Morris McDonald

NCIC: 19CI11PM1412PO11PI15

19 L 25 W IOM 14 Ref: 25 25 25
M 4 W OOI — 8 12 16

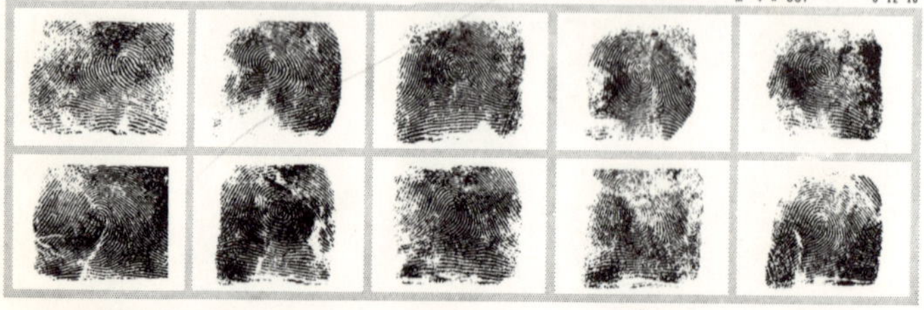

Photographs taken 1975

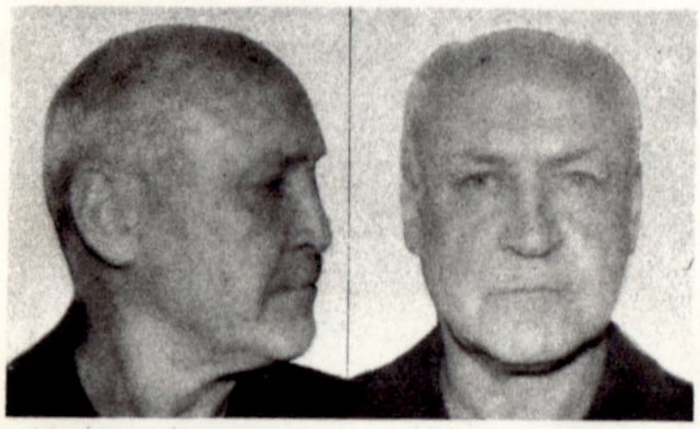

DESCRIPTION

AGE: 58, born July 14, 1917, Boston, Massachusetts
HEIGHT: 5'9"
WEIGHT: 165 to 175 pounds
BUILD: medium
HAIR: gray
EYES: blue
COMPLEXION: fair
RACE: white
NATIONALITY: American
OCCUPATIONS: laborer, truck driver
SCARS AND MARKS: pockmark on right cheek, scar on right leg below knee
SOCIAL SECURITY NUMBER USED: 022-05-6671

CRIMINAL RECORD

McDonald has been convicted of unlawful carrying of firearm and assault and battery with a deadly weapon.

CAUTION

MC DONALD REPORTEDLY IN THE PAST HAS EXCHANGED SHOTS WITH ARRESTING OFFICERS AFTER ESCAPE FROM A CORRECTIONAL INSTITUTION. CONSIDER ARMED AND EXTREMELY DANGEROUS.

A Federal warrant was issued on October 6, 1975, at Los Angeles, California, charging McDonald with interstate transportation of stolen property, receipt and sale of interstate property and conspiracy (Title 18, U. S. Code, Sections 2314, 2315, 2 and 371).

IF YOU HAVE INFORMATION CONCERNING THIS PERSON, PLEASE CONTACT YOUR LOCAL FBI OFFICE. TELEPHONE NUMBERS AND ADDRESSES OF ALL FBI OFFICES LISTED ON BACK.

Identification Order 4693
March 3, 1976

Director
Federal Bureau of Investigation
Washington, D. C. 20535

Entered NCIC

I. O. 4688
2-10-76

BANK ROBBERY; CONSPIRACY; ESCAPED FEDERAL PRISONER

WANTED BY FBI

PATRICK JAMES HUSTON

FBI No. 4,734,627

ALIASES: Patrick Adams, "Pat"

NCIC: DO161615PO1610131413

16 0 1 U 000
M 21 U 000 13

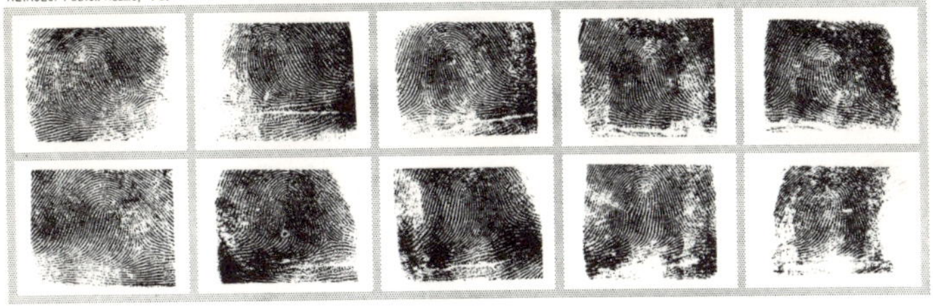

Photographs taken 1974

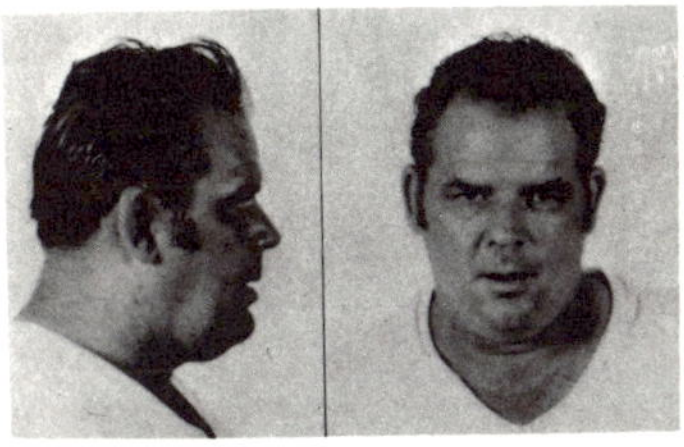

DESCRIPTION
AGE: 45, born March 5, 1930, Queens, New York
HEIGHT: 5'10"
WEIGHT: 225 pounds
BUILD: stocky
HAIR: black
EYES: hazel
COMPLEXION: fair
RACE: white
NATIONALITY: American
OCCUPATIONS: laborer, roofer
SCARS AND MARKS: appendectomy scar, scar on right knee, surgical scars from bullet wounds under upper left arm, middle of abdomen, area of left knee, left side small of back; tattoo: "In Memory of Mom" upper right arm
SOCIAL SECURITY NUMBER USED: 121-22-4022

CRIMINAL RECORD
Huston has been convicted of burglary and robbery.

CAUTION
HUSTON IS BEING SOUGHT FOR ESCAPE AND A BANK ROBBERY IN WHICH HANDGUNS AND A CARBINE WERE USED. HE HAS RESISTED ARREST IN THE PAST WHICH INVOLVED A GUN BATTLE WITH POLICE. CONSIDER ARMED AND VERY DANGEROUS.

A Federal warrant was issued on March 19, 1975, at Brooklyn, New York, charging Huston with bank robbery and conspiracy (Title 18, U. S. Code, Sections 2113a, 2113d, 2 and 371) Huston is also being sought as an escaped Federal prisoner as a result of his escape from the Federal House of Dentention, New York, New York, on March 16, 1975.

IF YOU HAVE INFORMATION CONCERNING THIS PERSON, PLEASE CONTACT YOUR LOCAL FBI OFFICE. TELEPHONE NUMBERS AND ADDRESSES OF ALL FBI OFFICES LISTED ON BACK.

Director
Federal Bureau of Investigation
Washington, D. C. 20535

Identification Order 4688
February 10, 1976

I. O. 4261
3-18-69

ESCAPED FEDERAL PRISONER

WANTED BY FBI

BENJAMIN HOSKINS PADDOCK

FBI No. 4,530,829

ALIASES: Perry Archer, Benjamin J. Butler, Leo Genstein, Benjamin Hoskins, Jr., Ben H. Paddock, Jr., Benjamin Hodgens Paddock, Benton Hoskins Paddock, Pat Paddock, Patrick Benjamin Paddock, "Big Daddy," "Chromedome," "Old Baldy"

20 L 9 R 000 18
M 1 R 000

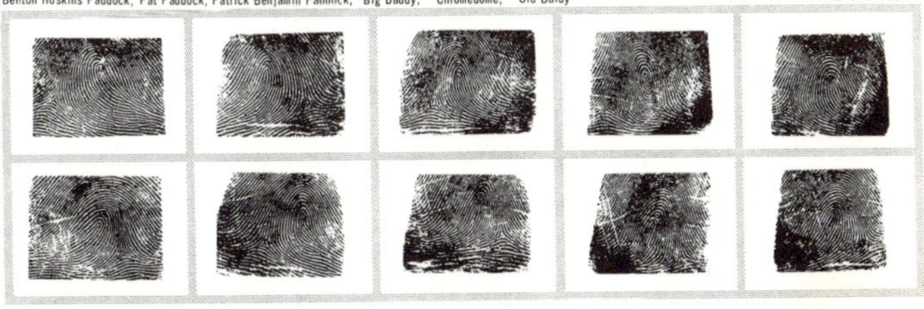

Photographs taken 1967

(Retouched photo)

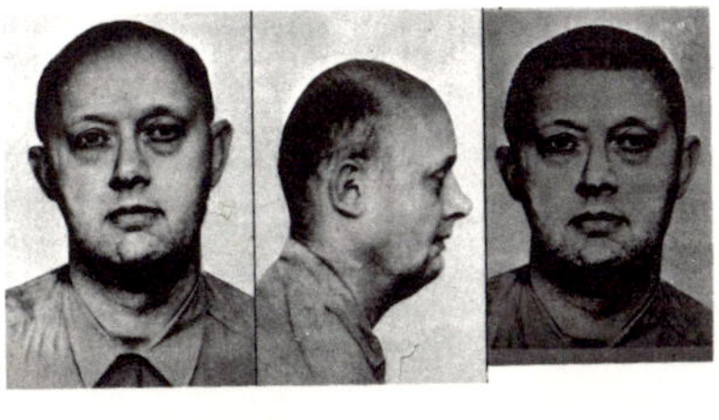

DESCRIPTION
AGE: 42, born November 1, 1926, Sheboygan, Wisconsin
HEIGHT: 6'4"
WEIGHT: 245 pounds
BUILD: large
HAIR: blond, balding (head may be shaved)
EYES: gray or green
COMPLEXION: medium
RACE: white
NATIONALITY: American
OCCUPATIONS: automobile mechanic, electrician, promoter, salesman, service station operator
SCARS AND MARKS: scar over right eyebrow, vaccination scar upper left arm, scar on right knee, birthmark right ankle
REMARKS: may wear glasses or contact lenses, avid bridge player
SOCIAL SECURITY NUMBER USED: 340-18-9361

CRIMINAL RECORD
Paddock has been convicted of bank robbery, automobile larceny and confidence game.

CAUTION
PADDOCK, DIAGNOSED AS PSYCHOPATHIC, HAS CARRIED FIREARMS IN COMMISSION OF BANK ROBBERIES. HE REPORTEDLY HAS SUICIDAL TENDENCIES AND SHOULD BE CONSIDERED ARMED AND VERY DANGEROUS.

A Federal warrant was issued on February 3, 1969, at El Paso, Texas, charging Paddock with violation of Escape and Rescue Statute (Title 18, U. S. Code, Section 751a).

IF YOU HAVE INFORMATION CONCERNING THIS PERSON, PLEASE CONTACT YOUR LOCAL FBI OFFICE. TELEPHONE NUMBERS AND ADDRESSES OF ALL FBI OFFICES LISTED ON BACK.

Director
Federal Bureau of Investigation
Washington, D. C. 20535

Identification Order 4261
March 18, 1969

INTERSTATE FLIGHT - MURDER; ASSAULT TO COMMIT MURDER

I. O. 4163
2-8-68

WANTED BY FBI

CHARLES LEE HERRON

FBI No. 313,926 G

ALIAS: Lee Jones

13 O 29 W 000 10
I 18 U 001

Date photograph taken unknown

DESCRIPTION

AGE: 30, born April 21, 1937, Covington, Kentucky (not supported by birth records)
HEIGHT: 5'7" to 5'8"
WEIGHT: 145 to 150 pounds
BUILD: slender
HAIR: black
OCCUPATION: clerk
REMARKS: may wear dark tinted glasses
SOCIAL SECURITY NUMBER USED: 402-44-7920
EYES: brown
COMPLEXION: dark
RACE: Negro
NATIONALITY: American

CAUTION

HERRON IS BEING SOUGHT FOR THE SHOOTING OF POLICE OFFICERS WHEREIN HIGH-POWERED RIFLES WERE USED. HE MAY BE ACCOMPANIED BY WILLIAM GARRIN ALLEN II, FBI IDENTIFICATION ORDER 4162. CONSIDER EXTREMELY DANGEROUS.

A Federal warrant was issued on January 19, 1968, at Nashville, Tennessee, charging Herron with unlawful interstate flight to avoid prosecution for murder and assault with intent to commit murder (Title 18, U. S. Code, Section 1073).

IF YOU HAVE INFORMATION CONCERNING THIS PERSON, PLEASE CONTACT YOUR LOCAL FBI OFFICE. TELEPHONE NUMBERS AND ADDRESSES OF ALL FBI OFFICES LISTED ON BACK.

Identification Order 4163
February 8, 1968

Director
Federal Bureau of Investigation
Washington, D. C. 20535

INTERSTATE FLIGHT - MURDER; BOND DEFAULT; PAROLE VIOLATOR

Entered NCIC

I.O. 4694
3-16-76

WANTED BY FBI

JAMES RAY RENTON

FBI No. 851,307 B

ALIASES: H. L. Baker, James R. Benton, Jimmie Lee Ford, Jimmy Lee Ford, Joe William Nock, Anthony Wayne Speck, Billy Wakens, Billy Wayne, Bobby Wayne, "Smiley" and others

NCIC: 18561013091256531412

18 L 1 R 9
M 1 Rr

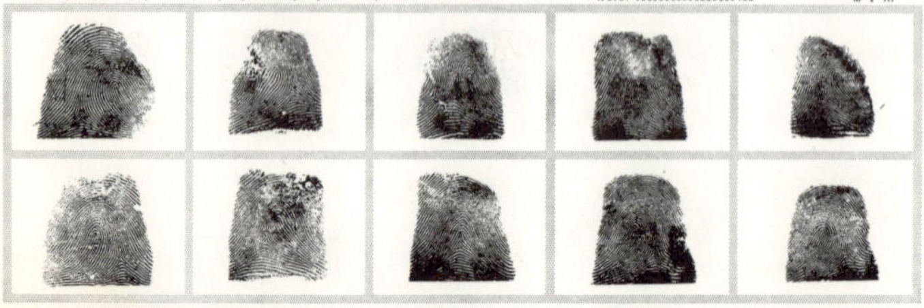

Photographs taken 1974

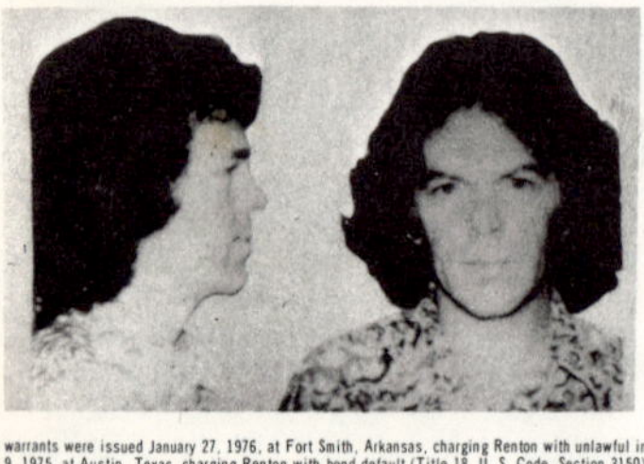

DESCRIPTION

AGE: 38, born December 13, 1937, St. Louis, Missouri
HEIGHT: 5'8"
WEIGHT: 150 pounds
BUILD: slender
HAIR: red-brown
EYES: blue (right eye discolored)
COMPLEXION: medium
RACE: white
NATIONALITY: American
OCCUPATIONS: advertising director, clerk, laborer, lithographer, photo-engraver, photographer, printer
SCARS AND MARKS: mole under right eye, large scar on right side of face, scar over left eye, scar on left index knuckle, bullet wound scar on upper left chest and bullet wound scar on lower back; Tattoos: wreath of flowers on left forearm, "J.R." on upper right arm, "Smiley" on right forearm, "RA 18458712" on left forearm, "G.N." on left wrist.
REMARKS: may be wearing mustache and small beard, dresses in western style clothing, reportedly an avid fisherman
SOCIAL SECURITY NUMBERS USED: 458-56-0454, 458-56-0456, 458-56-1454

CRIMINAL RECORD

Renton has been convicted of narcotics violations, burglary and forgery.

CAUTION

RENTON AND HAROLD DAVEY CASSELL, FBI IDENTIFICATION ORDER 4695, ARE BEING SOUGHT FOR THE MURDER OF AN ARKANSAS POLICE OFFICER. RENTON IS BELIEVED TO BE HEAVILY ARMED AND EXTREMELY DANGEROUS. RENTON POSSESSES AN EXTREME HATRED FOR POLICE OFFICERS AND IS SAID TO BE WEARING A BULLETPROOF VEST.

Federal warrants were issued January 27, 1976, at Fort Smith, Arkansas, charging Renton with unlawful interstate flight to avoid prosecution for murder (Title 18, U. S. Code, Section 1073); January 9, 1975, at Austin, Texas, charging Renton with bond default (Title 18, U. S. Code, Section 3150); and March 25, 1974, at Dallas, Texas, charging Renton with violating the terms of his parole from a Federal penitentiary.

IF YOU HAVE INFORMATION CONCERNING THIS PERSON, PLEASE CONTACT YOUR LOCAL FBI OFFICE. TELEPHONE NUMBERS AND ADDRESSES OF ALL FBI OFFICES LISTED ON BACK.

Identification Order 4694
March 16, 1976

Director
Federal Bureau of Investigation
Washington, D. C. 20535

INTERSTATE FLIGHT - MURDER, ARMED ROBBERY, ATROCIOUS ASSAULT AND BATTERY

Entered NCIC

I. O. 4657
3-24-75

WANTED BY FBI

ROBERT GERALD DAVIS

FBI No. 753,829 F
12 M 10 U 000 13
S 2 U IOM

ALIASES: Fred Billingsley, Potsey Davis, Kamau Karaumbi, Leon Smith, Carmu, Pottsie

NCIC: 121214CO13050914PMPI

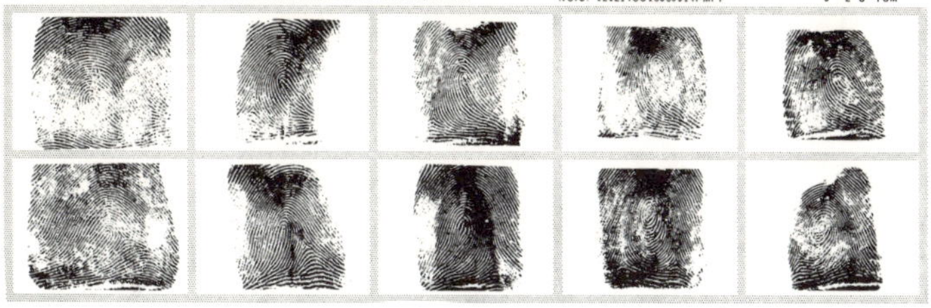

Photographs taken 1971 — Photograph taken 1974

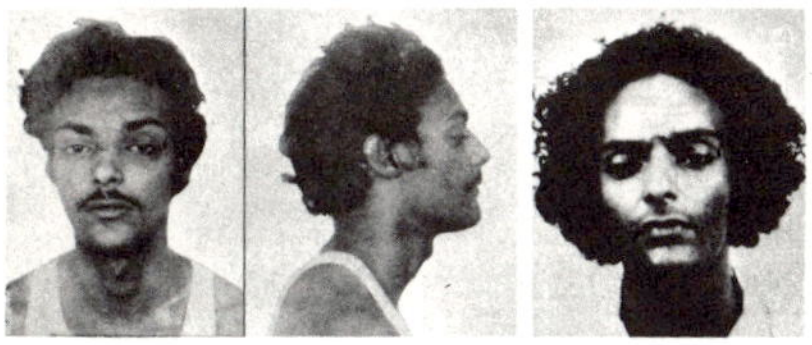

DESCRIPTION

AGE: 27, born November 15, 1947, Camden, New Jersey
HEIGHT: 6'2" — COMPLEXION: light brown
WEIGHT: 170 pounds — EYES: brown
BUILD: slender — RACE: Negro
HAIR: black — NATIONALITY: American
OCCUPATIONS: butcher, cook, floor waxer, hand crane operator, janitor, laborer
SCARS AND MARKS: two scars on bridge of nose, scar on outside of left eye, burn scar on left arm, burn scar on left side of neck, appendectomy scar, operation scar on right knee
REMARKS: may be wearing mustache, beard and have hair styled in ponytail
SOCIAL SECURITY NUMBERS USED: 140-38-9114; 140-59-9226

CRIMINAL RECORD

Davis has been convicted of illegal possession and sale of narcotics, possession of firearm and carrying a concealed weapon.

CAUTION

DAVIS, A REPORTED NARCOTICS USER, IS BEING SOUGHT IN CONNECTION WITH AN ARMED ROBBERY IN WHICH A 13-YEAR-OLD BYSTANDER WAS SHOT TO DEATH AND FIVE OTHERS SERIOUSLY WOUNDED. HE IS ALSO WANTED FOR THE SHOOTING MURDER OF A LAW ENFORCEMENT OFFICER. CONSIDER ARMED AND EXTREMELY DANGEROUS.

A Federal warrant was issued on August 7, 1974, at Camden, New Jersey, charging Davis with unlawful interstate flight to avoid prosecution for the crimes of murder, armed robbery and atrocious assault and battery (Title 18, U. S. Code, Section 1073).

IF YOU HAVE INFORMATION CONCERNING THIS PERSON, PLEASE CONTACT YOUR LOCAL FBI OFFICE. TELEPHONE NUMBERS AND ADDRESSES OF ALL FBI OFFICES LISTED ON BACK.

Director

Identification Order 4657
March 24, 1975

INTERSTATE FLIGHT - ASSAULT TO MURDER, ATTEMPTED BURGLARY

Entered NCIC

I. O. 4649
(Rev. 7-24-75)

WANTED BY FBI

BILLY DEAN ANDERSON

FBI No. 650,125 C
14 O 14 U Ref: 14
I 22 Tt 24

ALIASES: Bill Dean Anderson, Billie Dean Anderson, James Forster, William David Upchurch

NCIC: PO1414PIPIPITTTTCICI

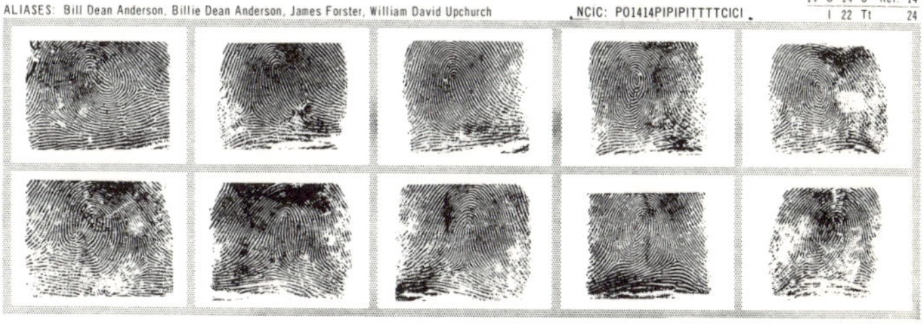

Date photographs taken unknown — Photograph taken 1973

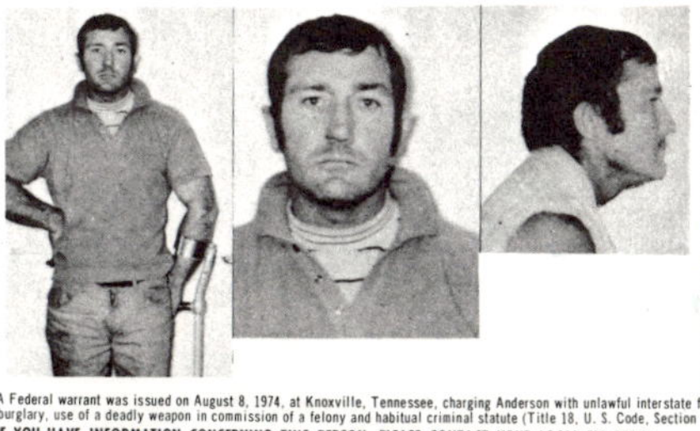

DESCRIPTION

AGE: 41, born July 12, 1934, Fentress County, Tennessee (not supported by birth records)
HEIGHT: 5'8" — EYES: blue or green
WEIGHT: 160 to 170 pounds — COMPLEXION: fair
BUILD: stocky — RACE: white
HAIR: brown — NATIONALITY: American
OCCUPATIONS: artist, mechanic, laborer, tree surgeon, farmer
SCARS AND MARKS: scar across nose, scar left side of forehead, surgical scar right side of stomach, surgical scar lower spine
REMARKS: reportedly wears braces on both legs and suffers from atrophy of legs
SOCIAL SECURITY NUMBER USED: 314-36-7484

CRIMINAL RECORD

Anderson has been convicted of robbery, carrying a concealed weapon and assault with intent to commit murder.

CAUTION

ANDERSON, WHO IS BEING SOUGHT AS AN ESCAPEE FROM A TENNESSEE JAIL, HAS BEEN CONVICTED OF ASSAULT TO MURDER LAW ENFORCEMENT OFFICERS. ON AT LEAST THREE OCCASIONS HIS SHOOTING AT INVESTIGATING LAW ENFORCEMENT PERSONNEL INCLUDED FIRING AT POINT-BLANK RANGE WHILE EXITING STOPPED VEHICLE AND WITH RIFLE FROM AMBUSH. CONSIDER ARMED, EXTREMELY DANGEROUS AND AN ESCAPE RISK.

A Federal warrant was issued on August 8, 1974, at Knoxville, Tennessee, charging Anderson with unlawful interstate flight to avoid prosecution for the crimes of assault to murder, attempted burglary, use of a deadly weapon in commission of a felony and habitual criminal statute (Title 18, U. S. Code, Section 1073).

IF YOU HAVE INFORMATION CONCERNING THIS PERSON, PLEASE CONTACT YOUR LOCAL FBI OFFICE. TELEPHONE NUMBERS AND ADDRESSES OF ALL FBI OFFICES LISTED ON BACK.

Director
Federal Bureau of Investigation
Washington, D. C. 20535

Identification Order 4649
(Rev. July 24, 1975)

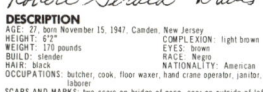

FURTHER READING

GENERAL BOOKS ON THE FBI

Lowenthal, Max. *Federal Bureau of Investigation.* Westport, Conn.: Greenwood, 1971.
Ungar, Sanford J. *The FBI.* Boston: Little Brown, 1976.
Whitehead, Don. *The FBI Story.* New York: Random House, 1963.

STORIES OF FBI CASES

Jeffers, Paul H. *Wanted by the FBI.* New York: Hawthorne, 1972.
Tully, Andrew. *The FBI's Most Famous Cases.* New York: William Morrow, 1965.

THE FBI LABORATORY

Berger, Melvin. *Police Lab.* New York: John Day, 1976.

CRITICISMS OF THE FBI

Schott, Joseph L. *No Left Turns.* New York: Praeger, 1975.
Turner, William W. *Hoover's FBI.* Los Angeles: Sherbourne, 1970.

The pamphlets below are available, without charge, from:

> External Affairs Division
> Federal Bureau of Investigation
> Washington, D.C. 20535
>
> *The FBI Laboratory*
> *Fingerprint Identification*
> *Know Your FBI*
> *99 Facts about the FBI*
> *The Story of the Federal Bureau of Investigation*

INDEX

Agent in Charge, 3
Agents. See Agent in Charge; Special Agents; Women Agents
Analysis of evidence, 34–48
Applicant squad, 32
Automotive Paint File, 39

Barker, Fred, 8
Barker, Ma, 8
Blood analysis, 40

Chemical analysis, 43
Clerical workers, 23
Computers, 15, 53, 55
Criminal offenses, 1, 5, 6, 8, 11, 13–14, 26, 32–33, 36, 39, 43, 46–48
Criminal records, 50
Criminals, Top Ten Most-Wanted, 32, 56

Dillinger, John, 8
Disaster Squad, 52

Evidence analysis, 34–48

Examiners, 23, 34–35, 36–40, 48
Explosives, 34–35

FBI (Federal Bureau of Investigation)
    and civil unrest, 11
    and communists, 11
    and Cold War, 11
    and World War I, 6
    and World War II, 8
FBI Academy, 16
    training at, 16–23
FBI directors, 6–8, 11–13, 32
FBI Headquarters, 15, 34, 53
FBI Laboratory, 15, 24, 34–48
Federal Bureau of Investigation. See FBI
Field Offices, 15
FINDER (Fingerprint reader), 52
Fingerprint identification files, 15, 49–52
Fingerprint reader, automatic, (FINDER), 52
Fingerprints, 23, 49–52
Firearms, 36–39

Floyd, Pretty Boy, 8
Fugitives. See Criminals

G-men, 8
Guns, 36–39
    firing of, 21

Handwriting analysis, 46–48
History, 6–14
Hoover, J. Edgar, 6–8

Identification Division, 49–52
Illegal methods, used by FBI, 11, 13
Investigations, 1–5, 25–48
Investigative squad, 32

Kelley, Clarence M., 11–13, 32
Kelly, Machine Gun, 8

License plate number, 53

Missing persons, 52

National Crime Information Center (NCIC), 53–55
NCIC, 53–55
Nelson, Baby Face, 8

Organization of FBI, 5, 15–16

Paint File, Automotive, 39

Recruits, 16–23
Resident Agencies, 15

Shoe impressions, 43–46
Shoe Print File, 46
Special Agents, 1, 15, 16, 19, 21, 24, 25–33
    procedures followed by, 31
    requirements for, 16
Special Weapons and Tactics (SWAT) team, 32–33
Surveillance, 31
SWAT, 32–33

Tape recorder, 2
Technical workers, 23–24
Tire impressions, 43–46
Tire Tread File, 46
Training, 16–23

Wanted persons, 53, 55–56
Wiretaps, 11, 31
Women Agents, 16

ABOUT THE AUTHOR

Although the author of almost three dozen books for young people, Melvin Berger is also a public school teacher, husband, father, and collector of antique books and microscopes. His special abilities in writing science books have earned him a number of awards for Outstanding Science Trade Books for Children.

Melvin Berger dives into his book research with eagerness. While researching for this book, he went out with Agents on actual cases. He also fired a gun for the first time, at an FBI range, where he discovered a new talent — marksmanship.